Beijing Express: How To Understand New China

BEIJING EXPRESS

HOW TO UNDERSTAND NEW CHINA

DAVID BAVEREZ

Westphalia Press
An Imprint of the Policy Studies Organization
Washington, DC
2017

This book was previously published by Editions François Bourin in 2017.

Translation by Graham Bushnell.

BEIJING EXPRESS: HOW TO UNDERSTAND NEW CHINA

All Rights Reserved © 2017 by Policy Studies Organization

Westphalia Press
An imprint of Policy Studies Organization
1527 New Hampshire Ave., NW
Washington, D.C. 20036
info@ipsonet.org

ISBN-10: 978-1-63391-625-8
ISBN-13: 1-63391-625-1

Cover and interior design by Jeffrey Barnes
jbarnesbook.design

Daniel Gutierrez-Sandoval, Executive Director
PSO and Westphalia Press

Updated material and comments on this edition
can be found at the Westphalia Press website:
www.westphaliapress.org

For Jérôme,
For André,

who remind us that people,
like civilizations, only die
if the living allow them to disappear.

"What comes into the world to disturb
nothing deserves neither respect nor patience."

Furor and Mystery, René Char, 1948

TABLE OF CONTENTS

FOREWORD

This book on China is unlike any other on the subject. It is not written by a researcher, an academic, or a politician, but by a businessman—an investor who has been living there for many years. David Baverez has also chosen an original format: Beijing Express is an imaginary conversation between the author and the new French President which takes place in the presidential jet as it flies from Paris to Beijing to which the new Head of State has elected to make his first official foreign visit.

David Baverez's task is to explain the "new" China to the President—the China where he lives and works every day. He attempts to get away from the fantasies, preconceived ideas, and clichés that Westerners sometimes foster as regards China. He wants to go beyond these and to take a close look at the ways in which the country has developed over the last decade or so. His aim is to convince the French Head of State that there are things to be thought about—even imitated—with regard to the methods being used by the Chinese to reinvent their country, especially by means of the Internet, social media, and artificial intelligence.

Of course, David Baverez is well aware that China is not a democracy in the Western sense of the word. Yet, it would be wrong to think that public opinion is not given its expression there: it is often highly critical and causes the government to change its practices and its policies, as in the case of protection of the environment. Since China is trying to bring the "Silk Road" back into existence by building ports, airports, railways, power stations, and freeways throughout the world, why not envision cooperation with China in building a "Digital Silk Road" so as to increase intellectual, technological, and cultural exchanges?

This book brings a fascinating insight into China's straightforward, pragmatic approach. It shows us a young, dynamic, optimistic, and enterprising society which is undergoing an unbelievably radical transformation which should make Westerners change all their old ideas about "The Middle Kingdom."

Westphalia Press
Policy Studies Organization

INTRODUCTION

Paris, May 2017. The new President of the Republic takes office. He knows that the paradigm has to change. He promised it during the election campaign and is convinced that it is the reason why he got elected. He also knows how fateful the first Hundred Days are—one has to start with a bang in order to show public opinion that the promised policies are being implemented without any watering down or prevarication. He knows from experience that what any new president does at the beginning of his mandate will stick with him for the rest of his term of office—Mitterrand going to the Panthéon, Sarkozy at Fouquet's and on Bolloré's yacht, Hollande walking up the Champs-Élysées in the pouring rain ... The question is: where to begin in order to radically change the French model? How to make a mark on people's minds, make a break with the past, and impose a new vision so as to make people accept the sacrifices to come? What example can provide inspiration for the targets to be set and for the means to achieve them? Should it be Germany as his counsellors suggest? "Look at Schröder's 2010 Agenda, the Harz laws ..." they say. After all, the first foreign trip of any newly elected French president is always to Berlin, isn't it? "No," he replies to his staff. "The French have had enough of the German example. And besides, the Rhineland model is running out of steam—look at the refugee problem, the rise of extremism ..." Then he gets an idea: "Which country has undertaken the most radical economic and social reforms of the last forty years? Which country has managed to rise, in only four decades, from the status of a poverty-stricken country to that of the second most powerful economy in the world? Which one has fundamentally transformed its system of production by placing all its bets on the technological revolution? China!"

The president knows that his idea will shock. China generally gets a bad press in France, being seen as an autocratic, deceitful, corrupt, and aging regime that is polluting the entire planet. But, as it did in the eighteenth century, it also intrigues and fascinates. It would really make people sit up if he went first to a country with which he feels he should create much closer and more frequent ties than his predecessors.

"Change of plan," he says to the Élysée general secretary. "Put off the trip to Berlin. We're off on a quick trip to Beijing. Angela will understand. There will be an outcry at the Quai d'Orsay but I don't care! I know the Chinese will appreciate it, and it will make headline news throughout the world. We're going to open a new connection: the Paris-Beijing Express. But find me someone by this evening who can tell me all about China during the flight— the China you don't see in the newspapers or in official reports. I don't want a diplomat or a leader of industry leader or a sinologist just someone who's not some sort of expert, but who lives and works there and who has daily contacts with the Chinese."

And so it was, by an amazing stroke of luck, that I, a mere investor based in Hong Kong, came to explain *my* China to the President during the flight from Paris to Beijing: how it could be a surprising source of inspiration for what would be, in France, the most wonderful "Cultural Revolution" of the early years of the twenty-first century.

SECRET—DIPLOMACY

THE PRESIDENT'S OFFICE

SHORT VISIT TO CHINA—MAY 2017

PREPARATORY MEMO—PRESIDENT OF THE REPUBLIC

TALKS—PARIS-BEIJING FLIGHT

From: France Stratégie

To: the President's Office—Preparation for a Short Visit to Beijing, May 2017.

Subject: Report on the lecture of Mr. David Baverez to the "League of Optimists of the Kingdom of Belgium" in Brussels, 15 March 2017, entitled "Nothing quiet on the Eastern front!."

As part of the preparation for the President's talks, please find below the most pertinent extracts from a recent speech by David Baverez.

May 2016: a lecture in Hong Kong to students in their final year at the Lycée Français International. Sixty students were present, all of them super-brilliant. They will all get their *baccalauréat* in a month's time, three-quarters of them with honors. To my question, "Who thinks that today's world is wonderful?," only two hesitant hands were raised, only to be lowered subsequently.

July 2016: a finance class in Beijing during the summer session of the University of International Business and Economics (UIBE). Thirty-five Chinese students. Every day, they all breathe air with pollution well above accepted critical levels and consume canteen food of very debatable origin, at least according to my modest culinary standards. To my question, "Who thinks that today's world is wonderful?," 35 hands were raised immediately.

How can one explain such a difference of perception? How can one interpret the fact that there is a deep disquiet among the future Western elite and an all-out optimism among Chinese youth? Two diametrically opposed views of the future.

In the West, an old world is crumbling. This can be seen in two icons of twentieth century progress: the car and the television. These days, the average age of the purchaser of a new Citroën is 60, while the 20-year-olds are sharing a Uber vehicle—which will soon be driverless. In 2015, for the first time, the average television viewer—the housewife aged under 49—was replaced by a viewer over 51 years old. Canal+, the TV channel that was the symbol of the opening up of the market in the 1980s, is losing almost 400 million euros a year in France. Concurrently, Netflix projects that it will have over 100 million subscribers throughout the world in 2017. This new American "barbarian" proposes movies on demand, offering total flexibility to the viewer.

At the same time, seen from outside, China seems to be accumulating all the imaginable faults possible: polluted, corrupt, dictatorial, full of inequalities, indebted, and aging ... And yet, a new world is being invented there every day: all these shortcomings are being decried by Internet users, analyzed by experts and then debated internally by the Communist party which sees this as a chance to reform a system conceived as a living element which can therefore evolve at any time.

In France, priority is given to "dosing reform," and coming only once a wishy-washy consensus has been obtained from "social dialogue"; in China, it is more a question of "daring reform," by taking decisions—sometimes extremely restrictive ones—but those which favor the country's future development. The will to do this is supported by the four steps that are needed for the success of any profound change: acceptance, diagnosis, identifying the measures to be taken, and putting them into effect.

Today, China's unique model is in continual development, which has enabled it to carry out the most radical transformation since 1978. The priorities being put in place are directly linked to social issues reported daily through social media; the diagnosis is being left in the hands of experts from the 80 million Communist party members; debates between rival camps are always extremely lively. This is a long way from the false perception in the West—

that presents a monolithic image of the country—and reveals a form of internal democracy. The resultant measures aim to turn a threat into an opportunity, as in the case of problems linked to an aging population or the indebtedness of state-owned enterprises. Finally, when decisions are put into practice, this is being done together with an astute combination of planning and pragmatism, supported by an acute sense of timing.

In a lightly veiled criticism of the West made during a recent interview with the *Financial Times*, Jin Liqun, President of the new Asian Infrastructure Investment Bank, summed up the exceptional qualities of Chinese leaders over almost four decades in the following way: "Chinese leaders have vision, determination and guts."

It is these three ingredients that are shaping the destiny of the "Middle Kingdom," to the great discomfort of the West, which is always ready to predict its forthcoming collapse: in 1978, when it came to light how much development was lagging behind because of Maoist aberrations; in 1989, when the Tiananmen demonstrations posed the question of political reform, in 1997, when the Asian Crisis suddenly showed how dependent it was on Western capital; in 2007, when the subprime crisis in the USA brought about a sharp fall in exports, which were the main driver of China's economic growth.

Another 10 years have passed and there is now an even greater need for China to reinvent itself, since it is becoming obvious that the reforms undertaken as part of the "New Model" were unrealistic. Domestic consumption has indeed taken off, but, unfortunately, not enough to put right the deep unbalances of the economy—this will take decades, not years, to fix. The present team of leaders must correct the failings of not one but the two previous decades. This means constructing the foundations to underpin China's next 30-year cycle—after those of Communism (1949–1978) and of the return to the global economy (1979–2008).

Therefore, "vision, determination and guts" are needed more than ever. The advantage that the Chinese leaders have is that they do not have to look very far back into the past to find a mentor to follow. They only need to take Deng Xiaoping as their source of inspiration. It was he who was responsible for the "Transformation of China"—to use the words of his remarkable American biographer, Ezra Vogel.

The vision remains—that of putting the Middle Kingdom back into its rightful place: ranking first in the world and dethroning the USA in all sectors by 2049, so as to give full weight to the centenary celebrations of the seizure of power by the Communist party. China wants to regain the leadership of the world, which, according to government propaganda, was its status before the "one-sided treaties" imposed by the West in the middle of the nineteenth century. We in the West, however, situate the decline of China as from the time of the Renaissance.

Determination comes from "Mr. Deng," the man thrice rejected by Mao: in the late 1930s, after a stinging defeat at the hands of the nationalist army; in the late 1960s, right in the middle of the cultural revolution, because he denounced Maoist follies; and finally in 1976, once again ousted by Mao a few months before his death, even though he had recalled him 2 years earlier to save the country from going wildly off course.

Guts come from the same man who, once was holding the reins of power, never veered from his obsession: to undertake structural reforms that would allow China to catch up with the West, choosing its best recipes for success and adapting them to local tastes. This deep conviction came from his determination back in 1992 to speed up the pace of reform in spite of considerable opposition and the fact that 3 years earlier, the pace had been denounced in Tiananmen Square as being too fast. Since his death in 1997, his place in Chinese history is that of someone who is remembered for managing to gain unanimous support.

Such is the background. "Vision, determination and guts"—versus the political inertia of the Old Continent—need to be re-imported into the West, particularly to Europe and even more particularly to France.

This new relationship between the West and China was splendidly illustrated during a memorable week in April 2015, in two singular events. The first was Apple's announcement of quarterly profits of 18 billion US dollars, beating the previous record of 15 billion held by Exxon, the American oil company. Tim Cook, successor of the brilliant Steve Jobs as head of the Californian giant, had to apologize to an audience of stunned financial analysts for surpassing market forecasts by 25%. He said "We had not anticipated the potential of the Chinese market," which at that time accounted for almost a third of Apple sales.

In the same week, another record—of quite a different sort—was broken. Manuel Valls, the French Prime Minister on an official visit to China, left Beijing without signing one single trade agreement. This was unprecedented! It was after this trip that, in Chinese decision-making circles, France was unofficially given an "AAA" rating: "Alcatel, Areva, Alstom," three former world market leaders that had either been bought up or were on the brink of bankruptcy precisely because they had not seized on the opportunities offered by China.

The accepted equilibrium has thus been singularly upset at the beginning of a century that will turn out to be merciless toward those who rest on their laurels. After decades during which China has managed to take the best of the West as its inspiration, has not the time now come to draw from some of the virtues of "Mr. Deng?"

THE LAND OF HUMAN DUTIES

Le Bourget—Presidential jet—President's Lounge

"Please take a seat. Thank you for having accepted my invitation to come on this flight with me. I have asked canon Dom Pérignon here to express my sincere gratitude, so let us raise our glasses to the conversation we are about to have! There will be *saucisson* and rillettes coming too. Perhaps you've already heard that what I appreciate most in my advisers is concision. So, to begin with, if I asked you to sum up China in a word, what would you say?"

"Mr. President, the very same question was asked by John Major—then British Prime Minister—when he was at the Kremlin and speaking to Boris Yeltsin about Russia. The answer came back immediately: *'Good!'* Then John Major added, 'And if it were two words?' 'In two words: *NOT good!'* came the answer. This confirmed British diplomats in their belief concerning the amount of alcohol served for breakfast in the Kremlin under Yeltsin. The same response is true for China: it is both *'good'* and *'NOT good.'* What makes this analysis so fascinating is precisely that, whatever the field under discussion, you will be confronted with contradictory observations—some describing a country at the end of its tether, others predicting its inevitable domination of the global stage."

State of emergency, state emergency

"Let's get to the heart of matter right away. How is it that this particular Communist dictatorship has been able to survive when almost all others have ended up collapsing?"

"China isn't a dictatorship in the normal sense of the word. It has developed a unique model of governance—its own particular model which can be reformed, which is mostly based on competence and which is impregnated with a pragmatism primarily concerned with getting results.

Behind this all, we find the basic principles of one man, Deng Xiaoping, the father of China's transformation—principles that continue to inspire the Chinese ruling class. They can be said to cover three main themes. First of all, being in control. This means always speaking and acting with authority, defending the Party, having control over the army and maintaining a unified command structure. Secondly, having vision—pursuing long-term objectives and choosing key people for their skills. Finally, mastering tactics. This means setting short-term objectives within the line of a long-term vision, making sure you have popular support before taking radical measures, taking uncomfortable truths on board, fighting conservatism by experimentation, and pushing, consolidating, and then pushing again. In short, being courageous."

"'A vast programme indeed,' as my favorite predecessor De Gaulle would have said, but in what way is this a unique model?"

"Because it is these principles alone that make it possible to reconcile the contradictions that are inherent in a country the size of a continent. You probably think of China as a highly centralized country. In fact, it's quite the opposite. Centralized taxes only bring in a quarter of public revenues at the most. Most taxes remain in the hands of the regions, which are highly autonomous. The system is very like that of German federalism. And this is what encourages experiments on a local level, as in the special economic areas of Guandong and Fujian, which enabled China to make a speedy exit from the collectivism IN the early 1980s. But, at the same time, national cohesion has to be maintained.

You may well have three hundred different cheeses to federate, but China has to make sure that two million pigs are killed every day in order to feed its population!"

"That may be so, but I doubt if you could compare Chinese *saucisson* with what we're eating at the moment ..."

"In France, we passed the 'Macron law' which was presented as a centralized reform of the economy; one year on, experts from Euler-Hermès have estimated the real effects as producing 0.05% of extra growth. In concrete terms, it has merely led to creating 1,500 new jobs for bus drivers. In China, priority has been given to local experimentation which, if successful, will be extended to all regions. On the one hand, we have a top-down approach which is nowhere near everyday reality; on the other hand, a pragmatic bottom-up approach."

"Even so, I remember one leader of a Chinese province quoting a famous proverb to me: 'The emperor is far away and the mountain is high'—to make me realise that he didn't much care about decisions made in Beijing. Which reminds me of my long discussions with my dear friends from our own PACA region in the south of France ..."

"And that's why Beijing has also to make centralized choices that will then be adapted to suit local tastes. Take, for example, reform of the public sector in the 1990s when China chose competition over privatization as overall policy. At the time, all our Western experts were recommending the latter, including in Russia. Going against all preconceived ideas, the Chinese government quite rightly believed that the future development of the country would come not from moving protected rents from the public sector into a few private pockets but rather from increased competition thanks to new private players. It has been proved right, for today, 1% of the wealthiest Russians control almost ten times more of the GDP in their country than their Chinese counterparts in theirs."

"That's what partly explains why Russia continues to sink into decline. It's really not by privatizing airports and putting them into friendly hands that its system will progress, but by laying siege to all protected niches.

I must admit to having a certain sympathy for the Chinese people, who see the pressing need for a strong state which gets its legitimacy from its competence. Such a pressing need is a legacy of history, for the Chinese, perception is that whenever there has been a strong state, China has been strong; whenever the state has been weak, China has gone into decline."

"The Anglo-Saxons rave about the concept of 'core competence' with regard to businesses or human beings, which lasts the whole of their lifespan. For the Chinese, competence is only understood as valid at a given moment tied to an opportunity and is therefore called on to evolve over time. Hence the whole system of governance has a singular ability to adapt. What matters is the result: it only took 10 years in the 1990s for China to double its GDP per capita—which rose to 3,000 dollars—whilst the USA took 55 years in the early 20th century to do the same. Pragmatism is the order of the day: in Hong Kong, both the personal income and company tax rate has remained unchanged at 16.5% since 1997 when the territory was handed back to China. In France, may I remind you that a company has to deal with 233 different sorts of taxes and payroll charges? There is no future in being a tax lawyer in Hong Kong—most lawyers prefer to specialise in shareholders agreements of new businesses!"

"My dear friend, we are touching here on the limits of a democratic government which creates constraints that a strong state can ignore when it is looking to reform. Fortunately, that in no way prevents our democracies from being 'the worst form of government, except for all the others' ..."

"If I may say so, Mr. President, that sort of made-up excuse has no legal force in China. When the Chinese look back at the last 30 years of political life in our country, they point out that, when looking at cases since 1980 when Article 49.3 was implemented to force legislation through parliament, 60% took place only between 1988 and 1990, the two years when Michel Rocard was Prime Minister—our only true reformer. So, the key is not the lack of tools at our disposal for forcing through necessary measures, but rather our inability to re-invent our democratic model in order to get it moving again."

When I hear the word *démocrature* ...

"I believe you call the Chinese system a *démocrature*. I have to say that this attempt to combine *démocratie* [democracy] and *dictature* [dictatorship] in one concept sends chills up my spine because we all know which ends up the weakest of the two ..."

"I understand your reservations. But let me explain: the most significant development in China over the past 15 years has been the appearance of public opinion. It has come to light through the rise of social media. Not only did the government fail to see it coming but it has expanded even more rapidly than in the West. Almost two years ago, a journalist from the state TV channel CCTV had a baby that had severe breathing problems at birth. The child was saved by a surgeon who identified the cause of the malformation: the air of Beijing which its mother had breathed during her pregnancy. The journalist decided to make a 90-minute documentary about pollution in China, entitled *Under the Dome*, a reference to the American TV series in which the population lives imprisoned under a glass dome. This remarkable film showed that Chinese experts had all the necessary data about pollution at their disposal and the information it uncovered was so detailed that it soon became obvious that it had had government blessing. Over only one weekend of its being shown on the Internet, the video was viewed almost 160 million times! The following Monday, the journalist was received by the Minister of the Environment who congratulated her and treated her like a national heroine. On the Tuesday, the video was officially censored and disappeared from the Chinese web ..."

"That's exactly what I was saying—it doesn't surprise me, coming from a dictatorship like that!"

"No! This is the perfect example of *démocrature*: the government has identified pollution as public enemy number one, as pilloried on the social media, but then buries negationist points of view out of hand. It signals to the population that it has heard the message and has taken note of its demands. That is the democratic side, illustrated by a cyber-democracy that the government cannot now strangle. On the other hand, putting corrective— and often unpopular—measures into effect is the business of experts and cannot run the risk of being debated by mere Internet surfers. That is the dictatorial side. But you can't simply put the label of 'dictatorship' on a system that today allows 80 million of its people to travel abroad every year and to come back and talk freely to their friends and families about the experiences they had during their trip."

"I fear you may be more than a little naive. I think the late lamented Edgar Faure may have had the last word on this when he said: 'Human rights: everyone wants to get involved, but in fact no one really gives a damn!'"

"The problem for us democrats is that we have trouble understanding how, in spite of a reduced level of freedom, China has made such spectacular economic and social progress. It goes against all the opinions and observations that have been put forward in the western world. Even someone with as brilliant a mind as Nicolas Berggruen, the founder of the *WorldPost*— and whom one could hardly accuse of totalitarian tendencies— summed up his thoughts after a recent symposium with the Chinese leaders in Beijing in these words: 'There is no contradiction between economic and social liberalization, and increased political control. Quite the reverse—it is a precondition for such liberalization."

"I don't trust the Anglo-Saxons. After the fall of the Berlin Wall, they paraded around with the so-called 'Washington Consensus' and now they want to us to swallow the 'Beijing Paradox.'"

"Perhaps you'd prefer the celebrated sinologist Simon Leys? In the early 70s, he was the first—and the most virulent—of Western intellectuals to condemn the atrocities of the Cultural Revolution. For this he was held in contempt by all left-wing thinkers of the time. For the record, when Mao died, your predecessor, Valery Giscard d'Estaing thought it appropriate to issue this statement: 'A beacon of mankind has been extinguished'! Getting back to Simon Leys, he explains clearly that China is not seen by its people as a country with geographical frontiers, but as a religion stretching worldwide: 'China is a religion for the Chinese people; China is not only a country, it is also a universal concept, a means for humankind to fulfill itself, an intermediary between man and cosmic harmony.'"

"Before then, Tocqueville had already said that 'only patriotism and religion can lead towards one single objective, the cohesion of citizens over the long term.' In China, you've got both of them—two for the price of one! I must admit to having a certain admiration for such a great attachment to one's country, one's culture and one's history. I'm impressed by this apparent cohesion in face of the outside world, and by the Chinese obsession with the condemnation of those notorious 'One-sided Treaties' imposed by the Western colonial powers in the 19th century, starting with the Treaty of Nanking with the British in 1842. They seem to draw from this national suffering the profound conviction that it is their destiny in history to serve as a beacon to the whole of humanity—an almost messianic mission that the government knows how to fuel to its advantage."

"In fact, Mr. President, the Chinese are not a religious people, at least not in the way we understand it. Buddhism, Confucianism and Taoism exist side by side, it's true, but you only have to visit the Lama Temple in Beijing to see that each place of prayer is above all a place where people come to find remedies for life's everyday problems. Religion is seen simply as material help in return for offerings. This explains the notoriety throughout the whole of China of someone like Shi Yongxin, nicknamed the 'Monk CEO,' who, with the Shaolin temple as a base, built up an extremely flourishing business dealing in tourism, martial arts and the sale of cultural souvenirs! The paradox is that the most deep-seated religious beliefs are to be found in members of the clandestine Christian church, estimated at almost 120 million people—one and a half times more than the number of Communist Party members! Getting back to the subject of civil liberties, even the weekly bible of liberals, *The Economist*, recently admitted that the Chinese people had no wish for democracy. The perception of China as the 'Land of Human Duties' is a direct legacy of Confucianism."

"I have occasionally tried to quote one particular Chinese proverb when talking to trade union leaders, starting with the CGT.[1] It is 'one mouth, two hands,' a way of reminding us that it is through work that we are made deserving of our pittance. But

---

1 The General Confederation of Labour, French Confédération Géénrale du Travail (CGT), is the leading left-wing union.

I haven't had much success, I must admit. France is the land of 'acquired benefits' ..."

"Unlike our own culture, for the Chinese, the counterpart of personal duty is that the system must produce collective benefits. They will only wait if they know what they are waiting for. They are prepared to make individual sacrifices if they can clearly see the collective benefits for the nation. The West hopes that, once a certain degree of wealth has been attained, democracy will prevail in China. Those who defend this theory even believe that the great day is not far off. By way of example, they use South Korea or Taiwan, whose transformation to democracy coincided with the rise in income of their inhabitants. However, unfortunately for these Western experts, I'm afraid that, when it comes to China, the point of reference should rather be Singapore and the strength of its state power ..."

"If I understand you correctly, it is exactly the opposite in France where 'the world is closed off and desire is infinite,' to quote the title of a book by Daniel Cohen, the economist. In China, on the other hand, unlimited collective opportunities make a large part of the population accept restrictions on their individual desires."

"It is precisely that, Mr. President. I would add that the major financial crisis of 2008 highlighted the limits of democratic systems when it comes to adapting to periods when there is some sort of breakdown. And breakdowns mean making painful but necessary choices to adapt to the new environment, inevitably to the detriment of some of the existing players. The great men who write history are not necessarily those who pay the greatest attention to the desires of the moment. Remember the way Henry Ford cocked a snook at the sacrosanct principles of marketing when he said, 'If I had asked people what they wanted, they would have said faster horses!'"

"I would never say this in public, but at key moments, direct democracy can even be dangerous. Brexit is a striking example of this: that vote, which should have been a rejection of THAT Europe—the one that my predecessors allowed to get bogged down in Brussels red tape and mismanagement, turned out to be a rejection of Europe as a whole. It's even more damaging in that we desperately need the British in order to reform the Old Continent! My hope is that the more Theresa May makes a fuss about her radical line of 'Brexit means Brexit,' the more she will try to take all the substance out of leaving the European Union. We know *perfide Albion*[2] well enough by now to know that it will always do the opposite of what it says it will."

"Perhaps the answer will come from one of the most innovatory men of the moment—the South African Elon Musk, now settled in California, whose ambitions include sending people on a weekend trip to Mars. In answer to the question, 'What type of government would you like to see there?' he replied, 'Direct democracy, the only system capable of avoiding corruption.' He also proposes that any law passed should only have a 12-month duration, and should be renewed only if it has proved itself. It is precisely the Internet revolution that must make it possible for people to take power into their own hands by expressing themselves directly about the big issues in society. A crucial factor for the rising generation. At the primaries which preceded the presidential elections, 50% of voters were retired people. At the mid-term elections in the USA in 2014, only 23% of 18- to 34-year-olds voted. At the Brexit referendum, only a third of 18- to 24-year-olds voted ... and 75% of them voted for *Remain*!"

"My dear friend, the fact that young people are deserting the urns reflects the generational choices of nations. I read in a recent report by France Stratégie that whilst the social and educational

2   Treacherous Albion.

transfers concerning the under-25s in France remained stable at 8% of GDP between 1979 and 2010, they rose from 11% to 17% for the over-60s. If we don't change this trend, we will be going along the same lines as Japan—a land of old people, governed by the old for the old ... I heard recently that the Japanese authorities are worried about road safety. To reduce the number of road accidents and persuade the over-75s to surrender their driving licences, the government is promising them free meal tickets for noodle soup!

You have to admit that my programme, which aims to dismantle driving schools' control over the issue of driving licenses—and which amounts to an oligopolistic racket—is much more forward-thinking! Getting away from the logic that is followed by the 'Young Peril' is an absolute priority of my administration."

"I'm sure that will please everyone. But one prepares for the future mainly through investment. Perhaps you could use your trip to Asia to compare how our so-called 'sovereign' fund—the Fonds stratégique d'investissement (FSI)—is placed with regard to the future, compared to its equivalents in Singapore—Temasek and the Government of Singapore Investment Corporation (GIC). On the one hand, our FSI looks rather like the A&E department of the Georges Pompidou Hospital, trying to patch up the 'broken arms' of our former flagships of the 20th century like Vallourec, Orange, CGC, Technip, Eramet and STMicro... On the other hand, Temasek and GIC look like a playground for the 21st century gems that are springing up all over the world, Young Xiaomi, Flipkart, Markit and Square. Quite enough to avoid the trap of the 'Young Peril' ..."

"Understood." (*The President turns to his economic adviser: "Édouard, when we get back to Paris, get me a report on all the public grants to start-ups, of which only 5% have really taken off after five years. And you will reallocate the money we get back from this to a fund managed by a real professional, which will only contribute to larger fundraising for businesses that have really succeeded. So that we stop them having to relocate to California in order to finance their growth. The French government funding the losers, while American investors pocket the capital gains from our winning French brains, has to stop! And if Mélenchon objects, tell him that we are actually nationalising the capitalists—that'll make him happy!)"*

But we are getting away from the subject of China. Let me ask you a rather DIRECT question: is President Xi Jinping a reincarnation of Mao, as a certain number of memos from the Quai d'Orsay seem to imply?

"Xibercracy"

"'Uncle Xi,' as they call him in China, is quite a fascinating character. He has declared that his ambition is to transform the Chinese economy but, of course, no one knows if his gamble will pay off. But the political organization he has set up and which he is constantly refining, is an unprecedented combination. For the moment, he is relying on four main pillars: a real and effective fight against corruption; a reinforcement of political strength unseen since Mao was at the peak of his power; a return to the geopolitical stage to bring China back to its pre-1850 status; and radical economic reform, although this is still at its stumbling initial stages at this precise moment in time."

"This Uncle Xi is some sort of superhuman if he is tackling so many things head-on."

"I arrived in Hong Kong in 2012, the year in which Xi came to power. At the start of the anti-corruption campaign, all the local experts that I met assured me that it was a stillborn project, like all similar attempts by his predecessors. At that time, the big annual convention of the Communist Party in Beijing in November was being commonly renamed *The Beijing Fashion Week* on the social media. The people's representatives proudly sported on their wrists the most expensive watches you could buy. To everyone's surprise, the campaign was extremely effective and hit where it hurt: 256,000 convictions within the Communist Party in the space of only two years! 177 deputy ministers or high-ranking officials investigated since 2012! From the outset, Xi got rid of two iconic figures: Liu Zhijun, the Minister of Transport, 'the man with 28 mistresses' and the happy recipient of kickbacks that came as thick and fast as the high-speed trains he provided the country with. And Zhou Yongkang, in charge of internal security for the Permanent Committee, the highest authority in China. He was suspected of having embezzled the trivial sum of 14 billion US dollars! This was the first time since the Cultural Revolution that such a high-ranking leader had been imprisoned."

"Impressive indeed. But isn't all that in line with a long tradition? The emperors put top civil servants in prison too. And remember Mao's obsession with plots which led him to carry out an almost continuous purge of the Party, right up to the Cultural Revolution. Isn't this a way for Xi to consolidate his own power? What's more, if I understand rightly, the economic consequences of the campaign are pretty serious and it has been contested in the Party ranks."

"Yes, apart from the witch-hunt, the campaign has had significant effects on certain sectors. Revenue from gambling operations in Macao has dropped sharply by almost half, from 45 billion US dollars—more than six times that of Las Vegas—to 'only' 25 billion. Proof that corruption accounted for almost half of its activities. The British pharmaceutical giant, GlaxoSmith-

Kline had to get rid of 40% of its salesforce in China once its dishonest practices concerning Chinese hospitals had been revealed to the general public! For Xi Jinping, the strategy was immediately given priority for two reasons: on the one hand, corruption proved to be one of the main hindrances to modernizing the country's economy; on the other, corruption mainly profited Western groups, either because it allowed them to sell their services in China—as in the case of the infrastructure sector—or because the misappropriated money was mainly spent on Western brands of luxury products."

"But that doesn't stop me thinking that the campaign served mainly as a weapon against any resistance in the Party and to nip it in the bud."

"Of course, especially against those on the side of Bo Xilai, the 'neo-Maoist' mayor of the city of Chongqing, suspected of having fomented a coup d'état in 2012 with the aim of putting power back in the hands of ultra-conservatives. Also, rumor has it that the weekend arrest in Shanghai in December 2015 of Guo Guangchang, the chairman of the Fosun Group, was intended to put an end to the financing of the Shanghai lobby which, under its 'Godfather,' former president Jiang Zemin, was beginning to prove a serious obstacle to Xi Jinping's maneuvers to put his supremacy on a firm footing."

"I can see the system is effective, certainly, as Guo Guangchang took no more than a week end und arrest to be brought back into line, but all the same, this seems to be in great danger of ticking all the boxes that mark a drift towards dictatorship."

"Mr. President, you're touching on the second mainstay of 'Xibercracy': the strengthening of political control. The family legacy of Xi plays an important role here. Between 1962 and 1978, when Xi Jinping was aged between 9 and 25, he only ever saw his father, Xi Zhongxun, either in prison or under house arrest. His father had been one of Mao's main right-hand men until he was repudiated in 1962 for having openly criticized the aberrations of the 'Great Leap Forward.' He only returned to power in 1978 when he was recalled by Deng Xiaoping and became the grand overseer of the first experiments in Special Economic Zones—in Guandong and Fujian—which marked the beginning of Chinese economic rebirth. Therefore, the image of his father that Xi Jinping holds in his memory is of someone who ultimately triumphed but wasted almost fifteen years of his life because he was unable to secure a strong enough political foothold to defend ideas that were economically right. Hence his strong conviction these days that it is necessary—following the reasoning of Deng Xiaoping—to make sure of absolute control of both the army and the Party before launching into any economic reforms."

"I remember being told at the time that the reason why Xi Jinping mysteriously disappeared for ten days before his appointment to office in 2012 was because he was negotiating control of the Military Affairs Commission before he took office, instead of waiting two years as tradition would have it. If I understand his strategy correctly, it was all about controlling the Party and the army before attacking the bastion of the major State-owned Enterprises, is that right?"

"It's exactly that. But I would add one more point—taking back control of the Internet. This was undoubtedly the biggest mistake of the previous—very conservative—leadership: they failed to anticipate the rise to power of the social media. For example, the WeChat platform now has 700 million subscribers! Xi Jinping's strategy has consisted in transforming this potential threat into an opportunity to develop his own handcrafted cyber-democracy. First of all, he solicited the whole population to denounce petty everyday corruption, so as to capture 'the tigers as well as the flies.' He also fostered frenetic online business, exemplified in 'Singles Day' on 11th of November every year. On this day, between 35 and 40 million men attempt to forget the lack of available women caused by the one-child policy, by means of a shopping spree. All to the advantage of Alibaba which manages the most frequented online shopping sites in the country. In 2016—in 24 hours—online transactions amounted to over 16 billion US dollars. Lastly, Xi is using new technology to gain better control over the population. The Baidu search engine can predict any crowd movement in a precise location just a few hours in advance. Very useful for preventing any rallies! And, unfortunately, for more than a year now, it is this police state aspect that has predominated in China, with a brutal and belated attempt to bring the social media under control. A sort of Big Brother which apparently is planning to introduce a rating system for citizens dependent on their behavior on the web. A kind of 1984 striking back!"

"The example of President Mubarak of Egypt has showed that it is no longer possible to simply cut off people's access to the Internet. These days, either the Internet makes it possible to remodel democracy by reconnecting with young people who have turned their back on politics; or else, means the spread of Big Brother. My fear is that China is falling into the second category."

"That's exactly the message that Edward Snowden carried with him when he fled to Hong Kong. Apart from the fact that the island was one of the few places that offered him at least temporary safety with regard to the USA, his arrival drew attention to questions on data security which finally came to be posed in China as well."

"Since you mention Snowden, I can't resist recounting a rather juicy little anecdote about the way the Chinese 'dealt with' his case. Our secret services told me that whilst Washington was demanding Snowden's immediate extradition from China, China—in order to gain time—demanded that an official request be sent in the name of 'Edward Snowden.' Snowden's lawyers were immediately alerted by Chinese authorities that they could not hold out for more than 24 hours, just enough time to negotiate his departure for Russia. In order to delay matters, the Hong Kong authorities informed Washington that, unfortunately, a detailed analysis of arrivals records at Hong Kong airport showed no 'Edward Snowden,' therefore he could not be on Hong Kong territory. It was only after the rescue plane was on its way to Moscow that the Chinese authorities confided to their American counterparts that they had identified an 'Edward J. Snowden,' but obviously he had nothing to do with the other one! An administrative subtlety working as a nice reminder of the problem of the middle name initial with which any foreigner newly arrived in the USA is confronted. Hats off to the Chinese diplomats in this case! But let's get back to the notion of political control. How can Xi Jinping claim both to control the Party as well as get round the machinery of government so as to take direct decisions?"

"You've put your finger on one of the most singular subtleties of the 'Xi system,' Mr. President. During the Cultural Revolution, all the children of the top leaders who had been arrested were sent off together into the countryside, as was Xi Jinping himself. In his 'great wisdom,' Mao knew that, in the future, the country would have need of its brightest brains. It was this generation of Princelings or crown princes—who showed exceptional solidarity—that Deng Xiaoping drew on for support when he returned to power in the 1980s at the age of almost 80. He asked each family to designate a representative who would be in charge of managing affairs. In the case of Xi Jinping's family, that person was his elder sister, Qi Qiaoqiao who was judged to be the most brilliant and whose fortune was estimated by the Anglo-Saxon press at several hundred million **US** dollars. These Princelings, who had had the benefits of the best possible education and were fluent in English, were the first beneficiaries of the opening up of the country to foreign investors for whom, in many cases, they acted as local facilitators. In this way, they enriched themselves royally, especially from the 1990s onwards, and now want to take political control at the expense of the established Party executives, notably the Communist Youth League."

"If they hadn't been helped by their birth, I would say that they are more like products of Xavier Niel's École 42 rather than of ENA[3]. This makes me confident about the potential for turning our own country around, if we draw on its real life-blood! But this Chinese system reminds me above all of our 'two hundred families' of the last century. Except that in China, I believe they are thought to total between three and five thousand. That must surely cause extreme tension in the highest state circles. What is the explanation for the fact that Xi Jinping is taking a huge risk in attempting to impose personalized power in complete contradiction with the collegiality that has been in vogue since Deng Xiaoping?"

"You're quite right to point that out, Mr. President. That's where any reference to Deng's legacy stops. Personally, I can see two reasons why this personalization and political hardening in China could well last: the first—as we have already said—comes from the need for profound economic reform which, sooner or later, will need the forceps; the second concerns political rivalry between the established Party structures, exemplified by the Communist Youth League, and the Princelings' clan."

"Doesn't this clash risk blocking the decision-making process within the Party?"

---

3   National School of Administration, French Ecole Nationale d'Administration (ENA), institute of higher education that traditionally prepares people for a career in the higher civil service in France.

"One day, I asked a good friend of mine from Russia to enlighten me on the new post-*perestroïka* system, and he was good enough to give me the following advice: 'If one day you should meet someone who claims to be able to explain the way in which power works in Russia today, tell him to take a little nap and, when he wakes up, he'll feel better!' This applies equally well to the Xi Jinping era. Historically, the Communist Party has never been monolithic and has always been the stage for fratricidal struggles between reformers and conservatives, between the 'Shanghai clique' and the Communist Youth League. Today, the arrival of the Princelings complicates the situation, which is turning into a "*ménage à trois.*"

"What you're talking about is a sort of Chinese take on a Greek tragedy. A real opera. Which, by the way, I'll be attending tomorrow evening in Beijing."

"Well, I hope you'll see as lively a show as the one currently going on inside the Party. On one side, you've got the League, the symbol of Chinese meritocracy which nurtured, for example, the present Prime Minister Li Kequiang and the former president Hu Juntao. It was openly criticised for the first time in the summer of 2016 as being a den of 'arrogant aristocrats.' On the other side, there's the Shanghai clan which knows it is under permanent surveillance since the sudden weekend arrest of the Fosun's chairman. Rumor had it that he was the group's main backer and was therefore indirectly financing Shanghai's resistance to the 'permanent *coup d'État*' instituted by Xi Jinping. As for the Princelings, they have been condemned by a large section of the Party—with the support of the population—as being 'crown princes,' the equivalent of our *fils*.[4] One of the consequences of Xi Jinping's choosing to draw mainly on the support of the Princelings is that he risks not having enough reliable supporters

---

4   "Sons of archbishops," implying nepotism.

within the Party in a large number of provinces. Such supporters are a key element of the Chinese power system. Hence Xi's temptation to centralize power even more."

"My dear friend, I hear what you're saying about Chinese federalism, which resembles the system set up in Germany after World War II, under pressure from the Allies who didn't want to see a recurrence of the centralized system under Hitler. However, I can see a contradiction in what you put forward. You say that this decentralization improves the competence of Chinese leaders who, before 'going up' to Beijing, have to prove themselves in the provinces. They even take a certain pride in this and do not hesitate to remind us that this explains why their system is superior to ours. At the same time, these fratricidal struggles you allude to are harmful to the smooth running of the country, and this implies a certain overall incompetence, don't you think? This hardening—unprecedented since the time of Mao—not only goes totally against our Western values but also reflects the weaknesses of a very ambitious policy of reform. As the Chinese proverb says, 'What you seek shows what you need.'"

"It has to be interpreted as a certain admission of weakness by Xi Jinping who, unlike his predecessors, cannot rely on solid support from a structure that is entirely won over to his cause. In the past, all the members of the Politburo had made a career for themselves within the Party and knew all of its ins and outs. Today, Xi is taking the very high risk of gambling on talent outside the Party—people who have gone from the political sphere to that of business."

"Regrettably, in France, our political talent has been being hijacked by the business world for over thirty years. A Swiss political scientist asked me recently why Germany had managed to keep sending so many great talents to the Chancellorship whilst, after François Mitterrand, the quality of our leaders has gradually deteriorated, culminating—if I dare say so—in my predecessor's mandate. I've always thought that the fault lay with the nationalizations and then privatizations of the Mitterrand era. He dug a trench between those who stayed in the civil service—bracing up the state-system—and those who understood changing times and went out into the big blue yonder, i.e. into managing large companies. The former were always at loggerheads with the latter. During this time, there was close collaboration in Germany between the business world and the political sphere—which was attentive to the needs of businesses. My concern today is also for our business leaders' understanding of the new world: out of the 430 directors of companies on the CAC40, only thirty or so—of which merely six are French nationals—have similar responsibilities in companies on the S&P in the USA, the FTSE in England or the DAX in Germany. It makes me wonder if our boards of directors need rejuvenating. Should I encourage them perhaps to visit Hong Kong? And I still haven't asked you how this territory will become integrated into the 'Xibercracy.'"

"There is no better place than Hong Kong if you want to understand how fast things are moving in the world. Only two years ago, everything looked rosy, but in 2016 growth was only marginal, hindered by the sudden drop in the number of Chinese tourists coming from the Mainland and the recent by-elections, in which everyone lost. The surprising rise of independentists illustrates the gap which has been created between Hong Kong and the Mainland, and between the young generation and the ageing tycoons who hold sway over their local oligopolies."

"Personally, I have to say that, like any Westerner, I was delighted by the results of the September 2016 elections when defenders of democracy polled almost 20% and even got 40% of the under-25 vote. It means that history is taking a direction in our favor. The Chinese are going to have to learn to abide by the contracts they sign. In 1997, when Hong Kong was handed back to China, they committed themselves to introducing universal suffrage in 2017 for the election of the Governor, so they cannot now say that the choice of governor is simply between two candidates designated by Beijing."

"Mr. President, I cannot agree with your analysis. In fact, my fear is that everyone ends up being a loser here: the pro-establishment—who are in the minority—remain prisoners of their support for the Chief Executive CY Leung, an incompetent puppet in the pay of Beijing; the traditional opposition has proved to be incapable of defending the aspirations of young people who want housing at affordable prices and are attached to sustainable development and the maintenance of a Hong Kong identity; finally, the localists—also known as the independentists—risk seeing their initial success fast turning into a Pyrrhic victory, since China is more likely to repress than to give in to pressure. And any confrontation with Beijing is likely to be largely counter-productive when it comes down to defending their ideals."

"And yet Hong Kong continues to be of great service to China, which would never want to kill the goose that lays the golden eggs."

"Looking beyond the current upheavals, a fundamental question emerges: how does Beijing envisage the Hong Kong model in future years? Whilst in 1997 Hong Kong accounted for 30% of China's GDP, today, at 3%, its share has become negligible. The problem for China is how to manage the urbanization phenomenon and produce sustainable cities. On this point, the 'light' governance of the island has reached its limits. Add to that the democratic demands of the Umbrella student movement and you will realize to what degree Hong Kong is on the point of becoming irrelevant in the eyes of Beijing. Finally, there is the third generation syndrome. After the generation of builders fleeing from communism in 1949 and the generation of traders of all sorts, has come that of the heirs—a generation of Ferrari owners."

"I have often been to Hong Kong and my personal conviction is that—aside from the questions you raise—the city will continue to surprise its detractors by its ability to reinvent itself. It will eventually avoid any 'Democrexit' and keep its status of 'one country, two systems,' provided that it manages to deal with Beijing. First of all, if you want to do business in the surrounding Asian region producing a US dollars 20 billion GDP, Hong Kong remains the only place where you can sign a binding contract. It's as if, in the USA, New York was the only place where to sign a valid contract. But then I think it's going to redefine its regional role, as a stakeholder in the Pearl River Delta Megalopolis project: to have 80 million inhabitants combining its financial and service capacities with those of software and manufactured goods from the neighboring cities of Shenzhen, Guangzhou and Dongguan. This will create one of the main world centers for the Internet of things. Personally, each time I visited Hong Kong, I always dreamed of bringing back to France a concentrate of its irrepressible energy."

"You're preaching to the converted, Mr. President. Every day I breathe in the air of this '21st century New York.' At the moment, they're building a bridge linking the city to Zhuhai and Macao as well as the Express Rail Link between Shenzhen and Guangzhou. The adjacent province of Guandong is already investing 4% of its GDP in Research and Development, i.e. twice the percentage of what the French are investing in R&D. Hong Kong is looking to make up for lost time in innovation by means of financial initiatives like the Alibaba Entrepreneurs Fund, which has been given 150 million US dollars to take local seedlings under its wing. I think there are surprises in store for us in the future with regard to the invention of new low-cost services, combining the best of the British legacy and new technology. Hong Kong will be the nerve centre not for start-ups—95% of which, according to statistics, still have fewer than ten employees after five years of operation—but for scale-ups, those real gems you mentioned earlier."

"So you see Hong Kong as an experimental ground on the economic and technological front, and not politically. I gather you don't see much future in the Umbrella Movement ..."

"True. I would bet on a long-lasting 'Xibercracy,' going beyond even the two usual terms of office of a Chinese president. Although it is certainly not held in high esteem by the West, the Chinese will ARGUE that Meisonnier, the most fashionable painter at the end of the 19th century, has today fallen into oblivion, whereas the Impressionists, who were widely disparaged in their time, are now renowned the world over."

"In my own particular field—that of politics—we venerate Churchill today as a monument of the 20th century, although in 1946 the British people rejected him for the premiership in favor of Atlee, an insignificant figure. Remember what Sir Winston is supposed to have said: "An empty taxi stopped in front of 10 Downing Street and Clement Atlee got out.""

"I would also add that Xi Jinping cares even less about his popularity ranking in the West because he has already managed very successfully to work towards something that is one of the reasons for his popularity in China—the only popularity he holds to be important: to put the country back at the centre of the world's geopolitical stage—the third mainstay of 'Xibercracy.'"

Our bulldozers, our rules

"Since you bring up the subject of China's geopolitics, let me tell you that I am very concerned about the rise of Chinese aggression in international relations, particularly in the South China Sea and even in Africa. Our secret services have passed me photographs taken by our observation satellites clearly showing that, in the China Sea, Uncle Xi is transforming desert islands into military airstrips. This, by the way, is one of the things that has convinced me to change my travel plans and bring forward my trip to China. We already have enough conflicts on our hands without getting into a new war in the Pacific ..."

"I think one has to start from this principle: on the domestic front in China, politics holds sway over economics. But externally it's the opposite: politics is there to serve economic interests and influence. Therefore, the more the West opposes the emergence of a multipolar government in the stead of the one bequeathed to us after World War II, the more China will be tempted to press its advantage, showing its capacity for imagination and creativity. Hence its setting up of the 'New Silk Road' and the new Asian Infrastructure Investment Bank.'"

"These two initiatives have not escaped me, but I tend to think of them rather as media buzz. Up to now we haven't seen anything very concrete ..."

"That's because we don't work on the same timeline. The New Silk Road, for which the Chinese have invented the acronym OBOR—for One Belt, One Road—is continuing a historical tradition in China, which, as far back as the 8th century, had opened up land and sea links with central and southern Asia, the Persian Gulf and eastern Africa. You may recall the famous voyages of Admiral Zheng He who, between 1405 and 1433, launched a fleet of over 100 ships that connected all the major

Asian and Arab ports so that his emperor Yongle—the third emperor of the Ming dynasty—could fulfill his wish to extend Chinese influence beyond the seas. The same reasoning is being used today. Xi has a thorough knowledge of Chinese history and he draws numerous references from it. What he wants from the OBOR is to develop—in a spectacular manner—land and sea routes linking China with central Asia, south and south-east Asia, the Persian Gulf, the Middle East, Africa and even Europe. One of the clearly identified targets is Iran with its 80 million inhabitants, heirs to a civilization dating back a thousand years. You have to go back to the break-up of the USSR in 1991 to see such a large population join the rest of the world economy, after four wasted decades. To our great surprise, we are gradually finding out that Iran is a country with an exceptional intellectual and economic potential. It is the country that has produced the first woman to be awarded the Fields Medal—the equivalent of the Nobel Prize in mathematics—in the person of Maryam Mirzakhani from the Aryarmehr University of Technology in Teheran. It is the country with the second largest proportion of government ministers with degrees from American universities—the first being the USA of course. It is the seventh largest market for cosmetics in the world. And I could add to the list ... Xi Jinping hasn't got it wrong. When he made a state visit there in January 2016, he declared that trade between the two countries, presently standing at 60 billion US dollars, should go up tenfold over the next ten years, i.e. more than the equivalent of current trade between China and the USA."

"My advisers know that nothing gets my hackles up more than the Iran dossier. Laurent Fabius did us a great disservice—showing outstanding arrogance and unparalleled incompetence. In 1992, 42% of Iran's trade was with the European Union compared to 28% with Asia. By 2010, the proportions had already reversed: 55% with Asia and only 19% with Europe. Of course, international sanctions had something to do with it, but that doesn't explain everything. If we look at what's going to happen in the next ten years, we might be led to wonder what cocktail the former Minister of the Economy must have been drinking when he exhorted French business leaders 'not to rush into Iran.' It is precisely our conservatism and our inability to understand changes in the world that will end up wiping us off the map for good if we don't react. Remember, in 1990, only Mitterrand was for a while opposed to the reunification of Germany and he was the only one to recognize the Russian generals' *putsch* against Gorbachev in 1991. And we were the only power to have almost scuppered the Iran nuclear agreement! I want a complete break with all this: putting France back in Iran—both commercially and geopolitically—will be one of the priorities of my mandate. But let's get back to this famous New Silk Road. Isn't it an attempt to provide large Chinese companies with infrastructure projects that are getting scarcer in China and to enable them to use their excess production capacity?"

"It is indeed a risk that the OBOR ends up being 'Our Bulldozers, Our Rules,' in other words, a means for bartering subsidized financing for economic and political subordination. In the years to come, we're going to have to learn how to discriminate between attractive infrastructure projects, such as with Iran or certain Eastern European countries, and some highly political projects, SUCH as in Pakistan or the former Soviet republics of central Asia. It was also ingenious of the Chinese to set up, in January 2016, 'their' investment bank—the AIIB or Asian Infrastructure Investment Bank—with an initial capital of 100 billion US dollars, and to have attracted shareholders from fifty or so countries, including almost all European ones. Only the USA, Japan, Canada, Mexico and a few others decided to snub it. China is the leading shareholder with 26% of voting rights, the head office is in Beijing and its CEO, Jin Linqun, is the former head of the China Investment Corporation sovereign fund. The Chinese are definitely at the helm here ... In fact, they were unhappy with the work of the World Bank—almost half of the projects financed there never reach their objectives. For the Chinese, its approach is fundamentally flawed: the fight against poverty isn't a matter of social assistance programmes, but the creation of infrastructure which enables a country to develop its economy. This is the way of doing things that has prevailed in China since 1978 and which the Chinese leaders would now like to promote in developing countries. It is this priority given to infrastructure that has enabled China to integrate over 200 million migrants from the country into the cities."

"I have to admit I feel quite close to their philosophy. And I would add that this is precisely what is cruelly lacking today in regions like sub-Saharan Africa or the Middle East. My brilliant friend Serge Michailof clearly explains in his book *Africanistan* that these are the two regions which will pose the biggest threat to the planet during the next decade: 300 million newcomers on the labor market, i.e. the equivalent of the population of the USA, without any qualifications or any chance of being integrated into the world economy given the absence of local infrastructure, and therefore ready to let themselves be seduced by the calls of radical Islam and its terrorist groups. I realize that this is what China wants to avoid. We are therefore going to keep a close eye on what goes on in this new bank, of which France is a shareholder; what kind of projects it will fund, and how governance will be organized with the Chinese board and notably if China will seek to impose its laws on the other shareholders, as the USA does at the IMF, for example. If China succeeds, it could pride itself on having reinvented the model for financing development aid, whose Western formulae—the legacy of World War II—are now outdated. This new formula will be even more innovatory if it brings the private sector along with it to leverage the effects. We should remember that Asia has an enormous need for infrastructure, estimated at 8,000 billion US dollars in the coming years. And if such an economic development enables us to avoid any confrontation in the China Sea, it's surely worth trying, isn't it?"

"I'm with you all the way on this one, Mr. President. May I add that Xi Jinping has a kind of 'stop and go' attitude towards his neighbors in the China Sea. During the Arab Spring of 2011, because of financial constraints and its new-found self-sufficiency in oil, the USA took the historic decision to abandon the Middle East, and make Asia the focus of their external presence. China's first reflex has been to strengthen its position in this region, which has greatly frightened its neighbors who probably recall the consequences of the rearmament of the German navy by Wilhem II in 1905. We have also been seeing a period of calm at the same time, with renewed Chinese economic diplomacy in the area, as in the example of the AIIB. The last few months have unfortunately seemed to mark the return of a certain activism on the part of China in what it considers as its natural sphere of influence. It seems not to fear any of these initiatives ending up with all its neighbors coming into league against it."

"What's more, President Trump risks offering it up the region on a plate by rejecting the Trans-Pacific Partnership. Obama had already decided to leave the Middle East to Russia, which means we'll be clinking vodka glasses with *tovaritch* Vladimir for some time to come. And Trump is preparing to leave Asia to China. It's incredible how visionary Clemenceau was when he said, 'America is the only nation in history to have gone miraculously from barbarism to decadence without the usual interval of civilization.' In the meantime, we shall have to show great diplomatic prowess and raise our glasses of maotai many times to calm the expansionist ardors of our Chinese friends ...'"

The President then turns to his Head of Protocol: "By the way, Renaud, I hope you have done a clean-up of the menus of the official lunches and dinners … I don't want to see any giant chicken's feet, warm chimpanzee's brains, and above all, no sea cucumbers. I'm happy to make an effort, but there are limits! Tell them I'm on a diet or something."

"That reminds me of what the American film-maker Michael Moore said after Trump's election: 'In June, Britain voted to leave Europe. Yesterday, America voted to leave America!' He could have added, 'And China is getting China back,' the great China of pre-1850."

"My dear friend, I have to confess that the way in which China managed to turn the Philippines around in its favor, to the detriment of the USA, in spite of an unfavorable legal decision, remains for me a model of diplomacy. A fine snub for the Obama doctrine of 'pivoting' towards Asia! The USA is undoubtedly still incapable of understanding the cultural subtleties of any place outside its own territory. As far as I'm concerned, China's aggressivity in the China Sea is directly linked to its internal economic situation. If growth is really running out of steam, then, like others before them, the Chinese leaders will use the external threat to distract the population's attention. That's why Donald Trump's policy with regard to China is a source of concern—including for the Japanese, which explains Prime Minister Abe's insistence on being the first foreign leader to meet the newly-elected president, before going to Pearl Harbor to greet Obama—a historical moment."

"Did you know that, since 2006, Donald Trump had been trying in vain to register his trademark in China? He had been coming up against the constant refusal of the courts because a totally unknown local property developer had already registered the trademark 'Trump.' Only three days after his election, his lawyers were informed that their request had simply been wrongly worded. The name, given the size of the group, had to be written entirely in capital letters—'TRUMP.' Once this was done, the name was registered immediately. The underlying message is: you have the choice between seeing your problem solved within three days or blocked for years. It all depends on your attitude ... It's a safe bet that, culturally-speaking, the opportunism of an adventurous realtor like Trump will adapt quite naturally to the Chinese way of doing things. But one cannot totally rule out the opposite scenario, which would see a dangerous return to power of the neo-conservatives of the George W. Bush era. The proven inexperience of the new President in the diplomatic field reminds us of that of his Republican predecessor. That could once again give free rein to the line of thinking that led directly to the Iraq War, with, this time, the speeding up of militarization of the China Sea as a main objective of the arms industry lobby."

"Like you, I think the Chinese are bound to be able to woo Trump much better than we Europeans. The Chinese and the Americans will be speaking the same language, based on the sole principle of the balance of power. The more Trump publicly accuses China of all ills, the more he will take delight in private deals made 'Chinese fashion.' He will bear in mind that the USA's 300 billion US dollars trade deficit with China will above all benefit the American multinationals that have relocated their production. And that China holds almost 20% of the share of the American T-bills that are in the hands of foreign investors. This is a strong argument in favor of Beijing, at a time when Trump is envisaging the doubling of the USA budget deficit during his mandate ..."

"You will also have noticed that one of the first suggestions of his advisers was to review the US veto of membership of the AIIB, so that America can skim off a part of Asian savings to its benefit in order to finance the modernization of its aging infrastructure. A sort of Marshall Plan in reverse!"

"My dear chap, you've just give me an idea!"

The President calls over his diplomatic adviser: "Xavier, have the Foreign Ministry prepare something on 'the world upside down,' the upsetting of balances, the Asian issues, etc. I am convinced that the French want to understand." He then calls over his communications adviser: "Anne, unless you have strong views against it, get me on the national evening news when I get back from China—fifteen minutes on the new international scene. I can see you're pouting, but I insist; it will be another way of showing to what extent we have to reform our country."

"If I may, Mr. President, I should like to say that you could take the opportunity to allude to the last summit of the APEC—the Asia-Pacific Economic Cooperation—in 2016, when China established itself—standing against the USA—as the unlikely defender of free trade, globalization and COP 21! And mention as well that in a recent survey carried out in Africa, the majority of people questioned considered that the Chinese model was more conducive to the development of African countries than the American model. This point of view has been upheld for a decade by the President of Rwanda, Paul Kagame, and we all know that he has been putting it into practice with positive results."

"I fear the 9th of November is a date that will go down in history for two reasons: for the fall of the Berlin Wall in 1989 and for the election of Trump in 2016, marking the return to 'walls'—not only the ones against Mexican immigrants, but also the invisible ones that divide minorities, races, the rich and the poor. I know Trump is always saying he likes to build but, this time, he's on the wrong track. You mentioned a while back that Chinese activism on the international stage would depend on their economic situation on the home front. But China is already in sharp decline, isn't it, if I am to believe the figures I've been shown?"

"Mr. President, don't waste your time drawing conclusions from the quarterly Chinese GDP figures. The figures are wrong, by their very nature. They are published two weeks after the end of each quarter, something which no other country in the world manages to do. Leave it to the world stock markets to get worked up over them. And beware of experts who propose as an alternative the 'Li Keqiang' index—named after the Prime Minister—which gives a synthesis of so-called real data, such as electricity consumption or freight volumes. That index takes little account of the booming service sector and is therefore an underestimation of how the economy is really doing."

"Let's get back to your famous pillars, my friend. You mentioned four but we have only talked about three. The remaining one is economic reform, notably reform of the main State-owned Enterprises. According to what I've been told, it's as if we were in that play by Samuel Beckett—all of us waiting for Godot ..."

The impotent lover

"Do you remember that song *La bonne du curé* [5] by Annie Cordy, Mr. President?"

"Of course I do—probably the greatest contribution that our Belgian friends have made to modern culture. But I don't see the relevance to 'The Middle Kingdom' ..."

"As the vicar's despairing maid, she sang *'J'voudrais bien, mais j'peux point!'* [6]—just like a lover who can't get an erection. That's the phrase being bandied about at the moment in China, re-

---

5 "The Vicar's Maid"
6 "I'd really like to but I just can't!"

ferring to putting some order back into the large State-Owned Enterprises—the famous SOEs. Xi Jinping has showed himself capable of imposing a complete reorganization of the army and the Party, but he's come up against a brick wall with the SOEs. The promised radical restructuring—as had already been promised under Prime Minister Zhu Rongji in the late 1990s—has not taken place. However, contrary to what one might think, Zhu—who was also a great fighter of corruption—still enjoys great popularity in China. This is even if over the four years he orchestrated public sector reform, he brought about the sacking of between 35 and 40 million employees, i.e. a third of the total staff of SOEs at the time. This was to prepare for China's becoming a member of the WTO—the World Trade Organization—in 2001. But since the 2008 Great Financial Crisis, the atmosphere has changed. When the world financial crisis began, the SOEs were the first beneficiaries of the stimulus plan for the economy, which manifested itself by the granting of massive loans, which are today the main culprit for Chinese companies' debts, to the tune of 160% of GDP. Most of this manna from Heaven ended up in sumptuous infrastructures, ports, airports, high-speed railway lines and real estate investment, of which a sizeable part has proved to be unproductive. Currently, there are thought to be 50 million empty apartments all around the country. Bloomberg Intelligence has identified 346 'zombie' companies quoted on the stock exchange with a total of 500 billion US dollars of debt. And all this is still going on. In the first quarter of 2016, SOE investments financed by borrowing increased by more than 20% as against only 3% for private companies."

"Let me play devil's advocate here. You yourself said that the Chinese work over the long term. Let's face it, the business district of Pudong in Shanghai, built in the early 1990s, took ten years to fill up. Remember the British wartime slogan: 'Keep calm and carry on!' I met the mayor of Shanghai who didn't seem to be in any sort of panic just because his new Free trade Zone, mainly designed for financial services, is still empty three years after its official inauguration ..."

"I concede that point without any hesitation. It's true that everything is a question of time in that country. We mustn't forget that capital stock per worker is still only at 20% of the American level and 25% of the Korean one. Bear in mind that, in 2010, a third of all households had no toilets or running water and almost half had no bathroom or kitchen. This is why, to make up for lost time, between 2011 and 2013, China produced practically the same amount of cement as the USA did during the whole of the 20th century!"

The President turns to his economic adviser: "Did you hear that, Édouard? In three years, as much cement produced in China as was produced in a century by the USA. We're going to have to revise the way we look at the energy of that country ..."

"My dear chap, we must obviously concede that the Chinese have a true long-term vision of reform and economic transformation. However, they are just taking inspiration from their Japanese neighbors in this respect. I recently met someone who had a great effect on me—Masayoshi Son, the President and founder of the Softbank group. He spent a whole afternoon sharing with me his vision of the information revolution ... right up to 2300! Fascinating! A sort of extraterrestrial in today's business world!"

"Perhaps, Mr. President, it would surprise you to learn that the Chinese take more account of the Korean model than the Japanese one. Korea has brought its GDP per inhabitant from 25% of the American level in 1980 up to 70% today. The South Korean miracle is built on increases in productivity that are still far above those of Chinese giants such as Sinopec or State Grid Corporation with their 1.4 and 1.7 million employees respectively.

Korea has also focused its efforts on industrialization whilst China has been concentrating on urbanization, which doesn't offer the same long-term prospects."

"Don't you think that the 2017 renewal of the seven members of the standing Committee of the Politburo—the people who effectively govern the country—will make things clearer as far as reform is concerned and the direction it will take? This game of musical chairs is sure to be extremely risky for the whole world over the next twelve months."

"That's true. To take an optimistic point of view, Xi Jinping is expecting to gain a new mandate and, in homage to his father, to further strengthen his control over the Party, within which the representatives of the SOEs and their accomplices play an important part. In the meantime, he's going to get rid of six million jobs in the steel and cement industries during the next three years. He can continue to depend on the exceptional dynamism of the private sector in which half the companies were founded less than five years ago. These businesses now count for two-thirds of the economy, 80% of jobs in urban areas, two-thirds of investment and 90% of exports, but only 30% of bank lending."

"On that subject, I have the impression that the top managers of our large groups, including those seated behind us in this plane, continue to underestimate the managerial qualities of Chinese private companies. I remember, back in the 1980s, meeting Chinese business leaders who were almost all former members of the armed forces, probably because they were thought to be the best people to head up tens of thousands of employees. Since then, with the opening-up of the country in the 1990s, we have seen the return of the 'sea turtles'—those Chinese who have spent time abroad, mainly in the USA, and who have imposed a different company culture in businesses, notably in financial matters. The large private groups like Fosun—whose leaders I met in Shanghai—benefited massively. Then, what strikes me about the first decade of the 21st century is, in contrast to what happened in Europe, the way in which China has given birth to real national Internet leaders—in online commerce, social media and search engines—such as Alibaba, Tencent and Baidu. And these days I'm hearing about the beginnings of 'disrupters' like Xiaomi and DJI which, with their telecommunications and drones, are going beyond their frontiers to conquer emerging markets and even Europe."

"Mr. President, during your visit you will probably be meeting some of these new 'conquerors' who want to master state-of-the-art technology, whether it be renewable energy, electric and driverless vehicles, high-speed trains, robotics or telecommunications. You will realize that, through these companies, China means to play the part of world leader in all these sectors."

"Yes indeed, I hope I'll get time to meet some of them. I have been struck by the way *entrepreneurius chinesus* is developing at the speed of a forced march—especially since I read a recent bit of research done by two Italian historians that the Finance Ministry told me about. Thanks to the digitalization of all the tax archives of Florence since the Renaissance, two researchers, Guglielmo Baroni and Sauro Mocetti, have been able to identify the families that have been paying the highest taxes in Florence since 1427. Curiously these are the same families today. When you look at what's happening in China, one doesn't know what to think: is the fact that these Florentine families have prospered over the centuries a sign of great capital stability? Or is it proof that we are incapable of renewal, that the wheel of fortune here is Europe is blocked, that our capitalism needs new blood, whilst Chinese communism seems to know how to renew itself? That said, for family capitalism to develop, you first need families and, on that point, I have the impression that the Chinese model is in danger; given the consequences yet to come after almost thirty years of the one-child policy."

"I HATE YOU, MY FAMILY!"
[FAMILLE, JE VOUS HAIS!, A QUOTE FROM ANDRÉ GIDE]

The one Child, multiple questions

The President is given some urgent messages. I start to rise from my seat, but he gestures me to stay with him. He gives some instructions to be relayed to Paris, asks if the other passengers are comfortable, glances at his watch and turns toward me again.

"Don't you think it's time we relaxed a little before going on with this conversation? Let's get on to family matters by reuniting family members of the drinkable variety ..."

The President then turns to the flight attendant: "Miss, this empty bottle of Gevrey-Chambertin urgently needs to meet its elder sister Vosne-Romanée, which must be feeling very lonely having been left in the galley ... Would you be so kind as to bring it to us?"

"Mr. President, do you know that the Chinese are pouncing on the vineyards of Bordeaux because they have been turned away from Burgundy where the local saying was hammered into them: 'In the Bordeaux region, very little to drink but a lot to buy; in Burgundy, a lot to drink but very little to buy!?'"

"Thank you. I'll try to remember that and use it again when I get the chance. Before we were so pleasantly interrupted, we were about to evoke the way the Chinese view the family, and the disastrous one-child policy which has resulted in an aging population and what demographers call the gender gap—the imbalance between numbers of men and women in different generations."

"Never before has such a policy been implemented on such a scale and over such a long period. Officially, it was begun in 1980, but only had any real effect on the birth rate from 1987 onwards. 2017 marks the beginning of a phase in which the number of people in their thirties will diminish, and this will accelerate as from 2020. But this is only the quantitative aspect of the problem. Added to that are two basic trends in present-day Chinese society which will change social relationships profoundly: the massive rise of social media and the break-up of family ties. Among the many upheavals caused by the Internet, one of the most important is the passing from a vertical way of communicating to a horizontal one. Confucian tradition preaches the importance of hierarchical ties both in the workplace and within the family, built around top-down communication. The notion of duty implies obeying the orders of a superior authority, whether it be that of a father or an employer. Confucius teaches that respect of the young for their elders, like respect for rituals, is the essential guarantee of a harmonious society. 'The Master said, "There are few good sons and brothers to be found who wish to offend their superiors. No man respectful of his superiors has ever been seen to become a disruptive element. The honest man cultivates the root; once this is in place, moral order is born. Filial piety and respect for one's elders are the very roots of humanity."' Now the social media, on the other hand, crush any sense of hierarchy. Theoretically, they enable one to have an unlimited number of contacts. No more is it a question of relating to a 'strong tie.' On the contrary, numerous opportunities are created for exchanges with 'weak ties'—previously unknown contacts—even to the point where they become friendships that are more virtual than real. The other great upheaval is that of family break-up, which is also being accelerated by the digital revolution. What possible subjects of conversation can there be between parents in their forties and a one-child glued to his or her smartphone? Hence a generation gap which goes far beyond age differences. Traditionally, from both a historical and cultural point of view, the family has formed the bedrock of social life, but now only 16% of Chinese adults visit their parents at least once a week. They are following the same path as the Koreans: the percentage of elderly people living with their children has plummeted from 80% to 20% in the space of just one generation. In Shanghai, 84% of people over 65 admit to having no social life, despite impromptu dances being organized in different districts. This explains the fact that, if you order a taxi using the Didi Dache app—the Chinese Uber—your driver will probably be a grandmother. For her, it is the only way to meet people, and this is also a blunt reminder that the criteria for granting driving licences in China are somewhat subjective!"

"Well, at least it has the advantage of giving senior citizens something to do."

"Yes, but this is becoming so widespread that, in Shanghai, for example, city hall has passed laws to preserve the importance of family ties in the Confucian tradition. Parents can file a complaint with the courts if their child does not visit them 'frequently enough.' In his great wisdom, the legislator has not specified the frequency, which leaves the door open to any interpretation. The first version of the law even allowed for prison sentences. This proved to be counter-productive since no parent would take the risk of denouncing his or her child. Therefore, a recent, more judicious, amendment has provided for the possibility that, if parents are abandoned, the child's rating with credit companies can be lowered so as to curb the child's taste for shopping sprees. But, I assure you, China knows how to use the stick as well as the carrot: a retirement home in Suzhou, near Shanghai, gives shopping coupons valued at 200 yuan—about 25 euros—to families who visit their parents more than thirty times in two months, 100 yuan for twenty visits and 50 yuan for ten visits!"

"The Chinese are a bit late in seeing the advantages of our pro-family policy, which continues to be one of the greatest successes of France compared to its European neighbors."

"Yes, but you can expect them to adapt it and add their own 'Chinese sauce' to it: last year a Shanghai hospital was offering a brand new iPhone for any gift of 17 ml of 'high quality' sperm—something that has become a rare commodity because of the unexpected consequences of extreme air pollution."

"Perhaps I should try and go there between two appointments—for the iPhone. The Élysée is still making me use the ultra-secure Safran cellphone—I'm the laughing stock of my children!"

"To my mind, the biggest challenge facing the Chinese on the demographic front will be more qualitative than quantitative. All of us have been confronted by the behaviour of only children in our developed societies: they tend to be more egocentric, they are used to getting what they want more quickly and they are often less inclined to making any effort. This is already noticeable in a city like Singapore, where affluent young people deliberately choose quality of life over the work ethic which drove their parents' generation. At Hong Kong University, rumor has it that a large majority of students from rich mainland Chinese families pay clever friends from their native region to substitute for them and get a degree in their name. In the meantime, they go around in Lamborghinis improving their driving skills—the average age of people buying these cars in Hong Kong is 27!"

"In fact, we don't exactly know how society functions when it is based on only children who, from infancy, have received the full attention not only of their parents, but of their grandparents too—something that will complicate their lives in society. I have also noted that the divorce rate in China—2.7 per thousand inhabitants—is now approaching the rate in the USA. As a result,

I've heard that the authorities are envisaging the introduction of marriage contracts valid for only seven years and renewable by tacit agreement. Perhaps I should suggest that idea to our public notaries to help them swallow the bitter pill of their monopoly being removed!"

"To be sure, Mr. President, the pressure surrounding marriage is hellish for young people in China, above all for women whose parents are always trying to make them marry a 'good catch.' Add to this the influence of the social media and this obsession can lead to some amusing situations: Ant Financial Services, the financing arm of the Alibaba group, had the idea of creating Sesame, a system of personal credit rating based on purchases made on the e-commerce platforms Tmall and Taobao. They then created online dating sites—'White-collar Agenda' and 'Campus Agenda'—where young women post their photos, preferably in highly seductive poses. The only people allowed to send them messages are Alibaba customers with a high enough credit rating. This has caused an outcry among Internet users, who have accused Alibaba of turning itself into ... a brothel for rich people!"

"'Alibaba and the forty ...'—I can see now the slogan for the French market. Fortunately, we have already sold Meetic to the Americans!"

"So you see how the family is felt more and more to be a real burden, although it is supposed to embody the most fundamental values of society. It will also weigh heavy on the economy, with the '2 + 4' people—parents and grandparents—that the single child will have to provide for. How is this generation going to develop when its backbone is being dislocated? Against the background of a rapidly-aging population, this is a question that is bound to occupy sociologists in the years to come."

A China neither rich nor old

"What you say about demography doesn't surprise me. A few months ago, I had dinner with the President of the Nestlé group, Peter Brabeck-Letmathe, who told me: 'China will get old before it gets rich.'"

"In one sense, he's right. The over-60s are effectively going to go from being 10% of the population in 2010 to 30% by 2030, a jump of twenty points, which is an acceleration in the aging rate twice as high as in the West. But in China, aging doesn't mean not working any more. The low unemployment rate is mainly explained by the fact that the average retirement age is 50 for women and 55 for men. When you're in Beijing, you'll notice a large number of retirees in the street doing community policing for the good of the local population, and for a modest remuneration. I talked recently with a representative of the Hong Kong Ministry of Health and told him how worried I was about the fact the number of doctors had remained stable for almost 20 years. He retorted with: 'There is no aging problem. The only thing that matters is the period of dependency, which, on average, is statistically about three to six months before death, whatever the age dependency begins. Up to that time, people can keep working!'"

"Perhaps I should have invited some of our trades union leaders to join me on this trip ..."

"Anyway, that's what explains why, with less than 5% of GDP given over to healthcare, Hong Kong has the highest life expectancy in the world—85! People from Hong Kong love to remind one that, every year, Americans spend almost 20% of their GDP on healthcare, and that individuals spend up to 40% of their lifetime's expenditure on healthcare during the last two years of their lives! Asians prefer to prioritize the education of the up-

and-coming generation, as in Korea where the Tiger Mums dig into their savings to ensure their offspring have the brightest possible future. And the government knows well, by looking at the social expenditure of Old Europe, that it would end up bankrupt if it adopted our welfare system."

"So, to sum up, China is 'actively old.' Now I'm getting a better understanding of why the Chinese paid such an astronomical price for the Club Med! But will they be rich one day?"

Wealthy state, poor people

"Mr. President, I think the phrase 'Wealthy state, poor people' is the one that continues to best describe for some time to come the distribution of the immense wealth created in China. Chinese growth has been financed by the dispossession of two social groups: peasant farmers and savers. Peasant farmers have been forced to sell their land to property developers for extremely low prices; savers are seeing their savings rewarded by the major banks far below the rate of inflation. Therefore, the government can use this mountain of money as it chooses and at a very low cost."

"That reminds me of the Russian proverb: 'One must take money from where it lies, i.e. in the hands of poor people.' In France, we have always wanted to do the opposite and we find ourselves with a wealth tax which costs more than it brings in."

"And yet, Chinese savers haven't lost everything. The extraordinary 'wealth effect' of the real estate bubble, especially since the first decade of this century, has sugared the pill. This scenario was the driving force behind the expansion of the American middle classes throughout the second half of the 20th century and the Chinese, in turn, have experienced it—in an accelerated version as always—over the last twenty years. This movement has been accentuated by massive recourse to loans and because, in the 1980s, housing could be snapped up at ridiculously low prices, often being sold off by state-owned enterprises to their employees. Unfortunately, this came to an end in 2014 with the sudden halt in the rise of real estate prices whose level no longer corresponded to the real level of salaries. I would bet that, over the next few years, real estate prices will be increasingly volatile, which will erase a part of this 'wealth effect' and will therefore encourage the Chinese to reduce their consumption. More so since, at the same time, hanging over them is the sword of Damocles of the pension scheme deficit, estimated by the Academy of Social Sciences in 2014 at the trivial sum of 86,000 billion yuan, i.e. about 12,000 billion US dollars."

"On the other hand, my dear chap, I wonder if the Chinese GDP isn't being deliberately underestimated. Experts from our Ministry of Finance have told me that Chinese calculate it using methods that haven't changed since 1993, and which apparently reduce it by at least 15%. I wouldn't be surprised if Chinese families weren't better off than official statistics indicate. I would guess that the key question that comes out of this for the government is to find the delicate balance between the development of domestic consumption and public investment in social infrastructure. I've been told by our embassy that the Chinese estimate that 1 yuan of public money invested this way could free up consumption of 2.3 yuan in rural areas and 4.1 yuan in urban areas. But I would bet that the government will go very carefully along this path and will in no way try to emulate our Western model."

"The real test, on the social front, will be the reform of the residence permit in cities—the *hukou*. It's been announced again and again that this will be put into effect, but it's only being done to a very limited extent. It would give social benefits and access to transport and healthcare to millions of migrant workers who, for the moment, are left to their own devices."

"But what I notice, my dear chap, is that the Chinese population, who have been imbibed with communist culture for so many years, seem to be accepting the spectacular increase in social inequalities and income gaps without rebelling against them. Maybe it's time to remind those Chinese billionaires—more and more of whom we see arriving in Europe—that they have to take on a social role in China."

"Your advisers will tell you that, on the contrary, they are escaping from their social responsibilities and will use as a proof the famous 'capital outflow' that the Western press makes such a big deal out of. That would be the warning sign of the collapse of China. The reality of the matter seems to me to be completely different: even if the flow of outgoing capital has speeded up appreciably in recent times, the 500 billion US dollars that go out every year only represent 2/5% of bank deposits. This is no general panic. Incidentally, this export of capital corresponds in part to commercial transactions or acquisitions of companies abroad. Of course, it cannot be denied that rich Chinese do in fact expatriate their families, most often to Canada, the USA, the UK or Australia, particularly in order to get a better education for their children. But, more often, they stay in China where they continue to work on the development of their businesses and of their country. For this economic and financial elite, attachment to one's country is extremely strong, certainly much stronger than that of French tax exiles in Geneva, Brussels or London."

"What you are saying reminds me of my recent meeting with Ren Zhengfei, the President and founder of the Huawei group. He was trained as a soldier and he has taken up the motto of General MacArthur when he was head of West Point military academy: 'Duty, Honor, Country.' Huawei's version is: 'Duty, Honor, Business, Country.' That may sound a tiny bit Vichyist to us, but, as you point out, it underlines a visceral attachment to the country, its history and its values. Do you think that's why the rich are not criticized on the Internet every day? Or is it because of government censorship?"

"On a daily basis, the criticisms of Internet users are far more focused on corruption and the distasteful origins of certain fast-made fortunes than on the very principle of enriching oneself, which is not only accepted but admired by the Chinese. Look at the example of Jack Ma, the head of the Alibaba group. He is venerated like a national hero! Internet censorship in China is political, not economic, exactly the opposite of our Western democracies. In Europe, we meekly accept a progressive economic censorship that is causing our media to disappear one by one, smothered by the Google monopoly which is gobbling up an ever-increasing share of advertising revenue without spending a penny on content. Therefore, democracies too are going to be victims of disinformation, either by means of free content diffused without the least qualitative filter, or by quality content which is naturally biased in favor of the private economic interests that see fit to finance it. Look at the mound of fake information that congested the web during the Brexit referendum and the American presidential elections."

"If you were to give me the choice between censorship engendered by the Google monopoly and that engendered by the Party, you would have to allow me to prefer the former. What strikes me about what we're saying is the degree to which everything in China is 'extreme'—a paradoxical situation for a country that claims to be the *Middle* Kingdom! When it invests in real estate or in infrastructure, it does so massively, even creating bubbles and phenomenal excess capacity. At the same time, its under-investment in the social sector is equally glaring. For years on end, the government manages to ignore a serious problem like that of air pollution, then suddenly decides to be one of the most ardent defenders of COP 21! Such turnarounds would hardly be conceivable in our hemisphere."

"No Planet B"[1]

"Mr. President, you are lucky enough to be at the head of a country on a human scale. China is a continent, a huge vessel that does not respond to half-hearted stimuli or half measures. For such a ship to move forward, it needs an atomic blast, radical programmes and revolutionary watchwords. Throughout its history, this is how China has functioned. The environment is a particularly striking example. Fortunately, this is May and you will only have to put up with a relatively low level of air pollution in Beijing."

"Indeed, I've had the weather forecast for the next few days—sunshine and clear skies during our stay. But how has the government let things degenerate to this level, even though toxic fog has been poisoning the life of the inhabitants of Beijing for years?"

"I think you might be surprised at how fast China is reacting, making a complete U-turn. It has become a priority after last winter when the protests of Internet users reached a threatening level for the authorities. COP 21 marked a turning point, but not the one which was officially highlighted. To my mind, the major event has been Bill Gates coming on to the scene, amid the heads of state. It marks the passing of the baton from nations to

---

1   A reference to Emmanuel Macron's warning to Donald Trump: "There is no Plan B because there is no Planet B".

the private sector. The nations only signed a non-binding decla-ration—they were not legally bound to do anything. However, Bill Gates has gathered around him thirty or so billionaires in the Breakthrough Energy Coalition. These billionaires are truly committed to financing and managing priority projects in the fight against global warming, and these actions will be height-ened by partnership with twenty or so countries through Mis-sion Innovation."

"I know about all this, of course. Particularly since I have inherit-ed the mammoth commitments of my predecessor in matters of energy transition: 50 billion euros of public investment between 2017 and 2022 to subsidise unprofitable alternative energies, like those wind turbines, half of which are not even connected to the national grid. Because of pressure from the construction indus-try lobby, we had to throw ourselves into a gigantic plan for the upgrading of energy efficiency in buildings, supposed to be the be-all-and-end-all of the fight against global warming. During my mandate, software and connected devices will be behind the most substantial energy savings. I totally agree with you that the 'energy transition' in Europe, including France, has been a com-plete failure up to now. But I still have some problems convinc-ing myself that China will manage to surprise us in this domain, given that it's been lagging behind in crucial technology."

"Would some concrete evidence help to convince you? Accord-ing to British experts, China reached its peak of CO_2 emissions in 2015. For the first time, during the previous year, its coal con-sumption diminished according to the Center for American Progress. It has committed itself to reducing its emissions by 60% between 2015 and 2030, whilst the USA plans a reduction of only 32%. What's more, the American commitment was made by the previous administration and we know that President Trump's entourage includes many climate change sceptics. Today, China's rate of energy improvement is nearing 5% per year: consumption is going up slightly whilst growth is between 5% and 7%. The Grantham Research Institute of the London School of Economics estimates that Chinese energy needs should only increase by 1.8% per year up to 2025, as against 8% during the 2000–2013 period. You could counter this by saying that it is still a very modest performance, especially since we know that, these days, China is wasting about 40% of its energy."

"I did indeed read that the International Energy Agency predicted, for the 2015–2030 period, an increase in volume of world energy consumption of only 1%, notably thanks to the measures taken by China."

"It has to be said that the Chinese situation on the environmental front betrays real urgency for action to be taken. The government puts an estimate of 300 billion US dollars per year on the cost of repairing environmental damage. The highest expenditure will be on soil and water treatment. Almost 40% of water reserves in the country are considered to be badly impaired. It will take decades to reconstitute groundwater tables. The Chinese Society for Banking and Finance estimates that 1,000 billion US dollars of investment will have to be raised in order to reduce carbon emissions in cities. Private funds will account for about 90% of the financing, two-thirds of which will be devoted to transport, notably high-speed trains and electric vehicles, 20% to energy efficiency of buildings, and 10% to solar energy. For the Chinese population, the main priority is the improvement in air quality, an objective which should be reached much more quickly in China than in other past examples—for instance, in London in the 1950s or in Los Angeles in the 1970s; two cities which were thought to have become irreversibly uninhabitable. What's more, China is now mobilising state-of-the-art technology, like the use of drones to measure air pollution at different altitudes. I am less optimistic about soil decontamination. It will take decades and, according to different estimates, will cost up to 1,000 billion US dollars. But, during your conversations, I'm sure you'll be surprised by the determination of the Chinese authorities to make their country a world leader in environmental technology, particularly in the electric vehicle sector."

"I see we've been reading the same things ... It has not escaped me that, in 2015 alone, China produced more electric vehicles than Tesla has produced in America since the company was founded. And Carlos Ghosn has already brought to my attention the fact that, in 2020, China will be selling more vehicles powered by electricity than by diesel fuel—and that diesel vehicles still occupy more than half the European market. Also, world solar energy production capacity today is ten times greater than what was anticipated at the Copenhagen conference in 2009, and we owe this mainly to China, which has given priority to it: 18 gigawatts put into service in 2015 alone, i.e. the equivalent of all existing American solar facilities. I also note that, in 2015, 160 billion US dollars were invested in solar energy throughout the world, i.e. the equivalent of all combined investment in coal and gas. This is the first time that emerging countries have invested more in renewable energy than developed countries, largely thanks to China's efforts."

"May I add, Mr. President, that China is going to mobilise its financial power to take world leadership in green industries. The Inesa company, for example, which makes LED-based street lighting, has a three billion **euros** fund at its disposal to finance the installation of their street lighting systems in about twenty European cities. Its remuneration comes from sharing out savings in consumption. Philips and Osram will hardly be able to put up any resistance!"

"Since the 2008 crisis, we have seen a new energy game coming into play. The big winner is the USA, at the expense of the Middle East. The Americans have a splendid expression for it: '*Shale: 1—Sheikhs: 0.*' In other words, shale gas and oil are bringing the oil Sheikhs to their knees. But European energy producers are ruining themselves in the tangle of an almost oligopolistic system which has prevented them from anticipating this revolution. They have had to depreciate their assets by almost 100 billion euros. Not to mention the biggest bankruptcy in Spain, that of the Abengoa group from Andalusia, which left its creditors crying over 9 billion euros worth of loans that had been wiped out. We urgently have to convince the Germans of the stupidity of their *EnergieWende.*"

"It is my belief, Mr. President, that the next energy breakthrough will be triggered by the appearance of ultra-low-cost models in emerging countries, especially in Africa. In Kenya, the M-Kopa company has perfected a solar lamp with a rechargeable battery which can provide lighting for a family for an initial investment of only 35 US dollars and a daily user's fee of 50 US cents. The future will belong to local networks distributing a decentralised flow of solar energy. In fact, the energy industries of emerging countries will be attempting to reproduce the telecommunications revolution: the cellphone enabled us to skip a whole generation of fixed infrastructure. The cost of a solar panel is estimated today at a tenth of the cost of connecting a house to the electrical grid. All this foretells an era of cheap energy, based on patterns far removed from what we are used to."

"And I am convinced, like you, that that the emerging countries—Africa as well as China—will be the big winners. They are the ones that will make the 21st century an electric century, with consumption of electricity growing twice as quickly as energy consumption as a whole. I have always thought that Jean-Louis Borloo, with his plan for investing 200 billion US dollars in order to electrify Africa, was using outdated reasoning. This is the time of local initiatives, micro-credits and mobilising populations, not the time for major programmes coming from above. But getting back to China's ambitions with regard to renewable energies, the amount of investment you mention is staggering. I am quite willing to believe that China, as a nation, could get the necessary financial resources together. But you tell me that 90% of this would be invested by companies, including the famous SOEs. Where will they get the money from if not from yet more loans? What I have read about China's indebtedness tends to make me think that, sooner or later, it will come up against a 'wall of debt.' But before we go into the subject of finance, I suggest that we move on to the Bordeaux. What would you say to a Château Gruaud-Larose? 'The wine of kings, the king of wines.' It would be the perfect opportunity to celebrate our trip to the Middle Kingdom and its legendary rulers."

The President turns to his advisers: "Your health, gentlemen, and I'm counting on you to make sure not a single drop remains by the time we land ..."

LAUGHING ALL THE WAY TO THE BANK

"Since we are embarking on the financial chapter, surely you must recognize that with the dramatic speeding up of its indebtedness since 2008—if I remember correctly, it's now got up to 250% of GDP—China won't be able to finance its development at the current pace for much longer ..."

"Mr. President, I think we have to go back to the 2008 Great Financial Crisis to appreciate the situation as a whole. At that time, the American financial system exploded because of the real estate bubble. But, very cleverly, the USA succeeded in turning the tables. They made the rest of the world foot the bill. They managed to palm off a very large part of these bad debts on to foreign banking systems, mainly European ones, and above all British and German. And they managed to push China—the only major country untouched by sub-primes—to revive the world economy by means of an unprecedented 4,000 billion yuan recovery plan, i.e. almost 600 billion US dollars. China then embarked on a two-figure growth rate, but at the cost of a very high increase in indebtedness, almost 100 points of GDP between 2008 and 2015, i.e. twice as high as in the West. According to the IMF, 63% of the increase in the world's money stock since the 2008 has taken place in China."

"Now I see why Donald Trump has decided, in turn, to speed up the level of public debt again in the USA!"

"Allow me to make an analogy here, Mr. President. Donald Trump is behaving like a five-year-old child in Toys'R'us who has been told that, today, all the toys are free. He has spent his life ensuring that he pays back as little as possible on debts contracted to build his famous towers. His advisers are now explaining to him that a public debt can in fact never be paid back ... So it's not surprising that he wants to open the valves all the way! In broad terms, I would say that this is the same logic that prevailed among the Chinese leaders in 2008. But this outpouring of public money will mainly benefit State-Owned Enterprises. The consequences are easy to guess: a sharp drop in the profitability of new investment projects, essentially devoted to real estate and infrastructure. It now takes almost 4 yuan to generate 1 yuan of extra GDP, whilst the ratio was nearer 1 to 1 before 2008."

"To put that into layman's language, you mean that Hu Jintao, who was President at the time, was doing his classic Chirac act: pushing the problem away by getting into debt and passing on the hot potato to his successor ... Hardly surprising that the two of them got on so well together!"

"Except that President Chirac is still exceptionally popular in France, whilst the Chinese have relegated Hu Jintao to permanent oblivion, with the specific reproach that he never undertook any reform."

"Which proves, my friend, that in China there are more limit to the naivety of the masses ..."

"Or that the desire for reform is more intense in China than in France ... If I may, Mr. President, allow me to get back to my line of reasoning. The four main Chinese public banks—Industrial and Commercial Bank of China, Bank of China, Agricultural Bank of China and China Construction Bank—account for almost half of the country's banking industry. Their balance sheets quadrupled between 2005 and 2015, reaching 80,000 billion yuan, i.e. over 10,000 billion US dollars. Officially, they are very profitable, with only 3% of so-called non-performing loans. In fact, according to the most respected analysts in the sector, they are largely under-capitalised, and the true ratio of non-performing loans is nearer 15–20%, in line with a country that is exposed to a serious real estate crisis."

"If I understand what has been written by Christine Lagarde, the director of the IMF, the non-performing loans in the whole of the Chinese financial system would amount to 1,500 billion US dollars, which could engender almost 750 billion US dollars of net losses. This figure is quite similar to the American banks' rescue plan in 2008, the famous *Troubled Asset Relief Program*, introduced at a moment when the financial world was in total collapse. As always, the problem comes from real estate. I believe that the Fitch rating agency estimates the creation of new floor space in China at a billion square meters a year, although demand is for only 800 million. What's more, a regional imbalance has come about because a number of these new buildings are being constructed in the secondary zone urban areas—called *Tier III* or *Tier II*—in which migration is now at a halt, and where prices are artificially inflated with regard to average local income."

"Remember, Mr. President, that the level of losses mentioned by the IMF includes what is known as *shadow banking*, which covers all the hidden financing granted to the private sector. This involves loan sharks who lend to private companies with cash flow problems at extortionate levels of interest, and these loans represent up to 60% or 80% of GDP. Now this financing is an essential element of the Chinese economic system, where the needs for working capital run over a nine or ten month period, as opposed to three to six months in the West. These lenders are extremely ingenious. In the past, they have demanded guarantees from the borrower that may include his car, his mortgaged property deeds... and more recently naked photos of his wife—which will end up being posted on the social media if the debt is not repaid!"

"Then there is no doubt that China will turn out to be the victim of post-2008 easy money. The paradox is that the more Western financial markets rejoice in the short term over high levels of activity in China, the more the Chinese leaders try to trim their sails ..."

"They admire Australia, the only country that has had twenty-five years of uninterrupted growth, precisely because it has been able to raise interest rates each time the mighty machine of indebtedness has raised its ugly head."

"I am among those who think that easy money will never be the answer to a crisis—it just prolongs it. But, during my mandate, I wouldn't like to have to witness the collapse of the Chinese financial system ..."

Cash is king

"Mr. President, I don't believe there is any risk of that, but this doesn't contradict any of my previous observations. China's external debt is only 3% of GDP. Furthermore, the experts who are crying wolf omit to say that bank deposits amount to the equivalent of 20,000 billion US dollars; that's almost twice the annual wealth creation in the country. They increased by a further 19% in 2015. This figure gives the Chinese financial system unparalleled liquidity. By comparison, American bank deposits are only a little more than 50% of GDP because of a low interest rate on savings and the existence of numerous channels of alternative investments. The strategic consultancy company, the Boston Consulting Group, estimates that the liquid assets of private individuals in China will double over the next five years, going from 15,000 to 30,000 billion US dollars—and this well is not about to dry up."

"If I understand you correctly, the so-called wall of debt is not a wall at all ... Or rather the Chinese have a very particular way of getting round it. It's a family matter, which must be settled within the family, without the outside world knowing too much about it. However, you only half convince me. Financial crises mostly originate from problems of banking liquidity, as shown by the Lehman Brothers bankruptcy ..."

"Mr. President, that's why, up until 2015, Chinese banks were under the regulatory obligation to limit their ratio of loans to deposits ratio to less than 75%. This didn't, however, get rid of imbalances in the system, but it provided time to put them right. Besides, the risk is not so much a sudden collapse of the financial system as a gradual impoverishment of Chinese citizens, since their savings are very modestly remunerated and siphoned off by the government to finance unprofitable projects."

"It's on that point that it looks to me as if government strategy is incoherent. You can't ask the Chinese consumer to spend more in order to support the growth of the economy and at the same time rob him of his savings in order to finance the increase in the public debt. So I ask the question: is time on the side of the Chinese financial system or not? Moreover, will those gigantic infrastructures—built with enormous help from loans—be productive in the long run? In France, it is obvious that the increased public debt incurred by my predecessors since 2008—at a cost that is acknowledged to be untenable—will merely have served to underpin a non-productive social infrastructure? Hence my question about China's ability to reform its financial system."

"It wouldn't surprise me if financial reform were not to precede a reform of state-owned companies. For that's the heart of the matter. Remember the previous reform in 2004. At the time, non-performing loans were already reaching 15% of the total commitments of Chinese banks and the state rescued them by injecting the equivalent of 30% of GDP into the financial system. But the growth of the following years almost wiped the slate clean. Today, the problem is that, in the coming years, China can no longer count on such high growth rates. As always in that country, transformation will not take place in a straight line, but will follow a somewhat tortuous path. It will have to deal with the gradual opening of financial markets, a tightening-up of monetary policy on quantitative easing, and with the development of financial technology—fintech—being put into operation by private players."

"Do you really believe in the freeing-up of capital markets in China? People around me seem rather sceptical about this ... The Chinese stock exchanges hardly inspire confidence. They are both highly volatile and regularly subject to doubtful practices, like the manipulation of stock prices and insider trading ..."

"Mr. President, you must surely remember that, during the summer of 2015, the Chinese government rocked the stock market boat by intervening directly to put a stop to runaway stock prices on the Shanghai and Shenzen stock exchanges where prices had doubled extremely quickly. Western experts saw in this a sign that the Chinese government would never comply with the rules of the financial markets. I'm not so sure. Today, the Chinese stock exchange is just a sort of casino where 80% of the listed companies are businesses in which the state holds at least 60% of the capital. Therefore, stock market prices have no significant link with the reality of either the Chinese economy or of private companies that are financed more by loans or self-financing than on the trading floor. In 2015, the government intervened to burst the bubble that had brought stock market capitalization up to 125% of GDP ... A level that was thought to be excessive."

"It's a better strategy that the one implemented by the President of the American Federal Reserve, Ben Bernanke, who in 2006 continued to maintain that the bottom could not fall out of the real estate market and that there was therefore no need to intervene!"

"I don't doubt it. His Chinese counterparts show more concern over the basic equilibrium of the country. That's why they saw fit to burst the abscess during the first months when it began to form. They did it in a directive manner, going against all market rules. But one has to admit that the facts have proved them right. This episode should make one realize, Mr. President, that at this stage the government is not ready to let market forces operate freely, and that it will take at least a decade to arrive at total liberalization."

"If we wanted to be objective, we would nevertheless take note that Western regulators have also intervened in the financial markets since 2008, to the point of keeping them at an artificially high level at the present time. People who criticize the interventionism of the Chinese authorities are less ready to condemn the interventions of the European Central Bank, which has nevertheless injected 1,000 billion euros into the markets. An unbelievable gift to the Eurozone banks to mask the volume of their non-performing loans, which, curiously, are reaching a very similar amount ..."

"The problem with quantitative easing is knowing how to stop it. That is the question facing the USA at the moment, but will also face the Eurozone at one time or another. It's also the major concern of the Chinese government. Even today, China is suffering from the excessive growth of its money stock, which has gone far beyond the increase in GDP. The government attempted to put the brakes on during the second quarter of 2015, but it got out of control again in 2016, with the granting of 1,500 billion US dollars of new loans in the first quarter, i.e. 15% of GDP. Debt continues to grow dangerously, much faster than national wealth creation, and this is untenable over the long term. Even more so in that the way the money is used leaves a lot to be desired. In short, State-Owned Enterprises are readier to spend it on real estate speculation than on restructuring their operations. But a reversal of this trend may be on the way. New combinations are being developed in which state-owned companies that are not doing well oblige their creditors to convert their debt into capital at a highly unfavorable ratio, because legally it has to be higher than or equal to the net book value, which can turn out to be very artificial. The first conversion plan concerned 1,000 billion yuan of debts, i.e. 150 billion US dollars. This can but push banks into being much more selective. You can expect to see this problem dealt with 'the Chinese way,' i.e. over time, but in a way that is painful for anyone who, when all is said and done, has been acting against the country's interests. For politics is never far away: there is often a confusion of interests, even connivance between the heads of State-Owned Enterprises and the heads of major public banks who are more often than not Party members and belong to one or another faction or alliance. This desire to restructure the debts of state-owned companies may also conceal the settling of old scores."

"I see what you mean. It reminds me a bit of the time when almost all the banks were nationalised in France ... However, there is one point on which my mind is not yet made up. I can well see how the traditional banks in Western countries are being attacked by new players who claim to practice the same trade and depend on new technology to foster, shall we say, the 'uberisation' of finance. But, given the very directive attitude of the Chinese government as far as finance is concerned, I can't see how it would let such players establish themselves, unless they see in them a way of making the large banks reform themselves ..."

"You're quite right, Mr. President. It is government strategy to encourage an increase in the power of private fintech stakeholders in order to foster the modernisation of financial operations. The government is counting on the web giants—Baidu, Alibaba and Tencent—to lay siege to the banking oligopoly. The payment-by-cellphone sector, for example, is booming. Alipay and Weixin Pay have already claimed 90% of the market for themselves, leaving the remainder to the incumbent state-owned organization, UnionPay. There is no better illustration of the technological boom of Chinese financial services than Alibaba which, with its famous 'Singles Day' on 11th November, granted one hundred million personal loans in one single day, something that no other banking organization in the world would be capable of doing. Therefore, Alibaba looks like becoming, in the long term, one of the leading global financial players. There's a revolution going on, but the downside is that this opening up to new models will always be rejected by foreign stakeholders, so that the immense amount of value generated in this way will remain in the hands of the Chinese. KPMG, which has produced a report on fintechs, puts Chinese companies among the leading five in the world. The financial subsidiary of the Alibaba Group, Ant Financial Services, is apparently already worth 60 billion US dollars. If you want to understand the potential of these 'new barbarians,' just look at... the sperm bank! After a promotional campaign that lasted only three days, Alibaba—yes, Alibaba again—managed to recruit as many donors as existing institutions manage to recruit in a year!"

"'Alibaba and the forty donors' could be a rather good slogan for when they arrive in France! But let's not get away from the subject ... Do you share my view that the modernisation of the Chinese financial system can only be achieved with currency convertibility?"

"The Convertible looks very nice!"

"Mr. President, now you're touching the most sensitive spot as far as Chinese monetary policy is concerned. Total convertibility of the yuan is an objective that is regularly reiterated by the government. But it is a highly complex operation. According to all the experts, it won't happen before at least ten years. China already won a huge victory in October 2016 when its currency joined the IMF basket of Special Drawing Rights, alongside the dollar, the euro, the yen and the pound sterling. Of course, the Chinese currency only accounts for 10.9% of this basket, as opposed to 41% for the dollar and 30% for the euro, but this is more than the yen and the pound which each account for a little over 8%. However, this doesn't yet make the Yuan an international currency. It represents scarcely 2% of global transactions. When Chinese Government bonds were issued in London in May 2016—the first offshore Chinese operation outside Hong Kong—the operation was promising. But if total convertibility were to be reached, this would make China part of world financial capitalism, which it is not ready for, precisely because the Chinese financial system is not yet suited for such a radical transformation. The strategy is to internationalize the yuan and the tactic is to do this gradually so as not to destabilize the country. The financial system functions in a sort of no man's land between a certain degree of freedom and the omnipresent apparatus of control. Cast your mind back to the devaluation of August 2015 ... But, as always in China, although the timing is uncertain, the determination is there and the aim is to make China a global financial power in the long term, able to compete with and even overtake the USA. The next decade will therefore see the biggest financial operation ever undertaken: the convertibility of 20,000 billion US dollars of Chinese bank deposits. This will enable China to reach a triple objective: to free itself from American domination, so as not to be held hostage as in 2008; to speed up the purchase of strategic assets throughout the world; and to diversify its liquidity under careful supervision."

"Given that it is the role of the dollar in transactions and international reserves that makes the USA the leading world financial power, isn't it a bit presumptuous to aspire to oust the USA from that position?"

"It took the USA almost five decades—from the end of the 19th century up to the Bretton Woods agreement in 1944—to go from being economically number one to establishing itself as the leader of the world financial system. China aims to make the same transition, but, as always with our Chinese friends, in a much shorter time frame. In their eyes, reducing the rest of the world's financial dependency on the USA must help towards creating a more balanced world."

"But China is already convinced it is the leading world economy, once the purchasing power parities have been adjusted ..."

"So it is not going to accept any devaluation of its currency that is not controlled, modest and regular, as has been the case since the summer of 2015. What they are doing is simply correcting the excessive 30% appreciation in value of the yuan since the 2008 crisis."

"I can well see the aim they are pursuing. Strictly speaking, it's less of a devaluation than a 'de-revaluation,' so as to avoid the trap that the USA laid for Japan in the 1990s, when the appreciation of the yen was too high and contributed greatly to the decline of the Japanese economy."

"Yes indeed, Mr. President, the idea is to allow the yuan to continue gaining a market share in global transactions at the expense of the euro and the yen. One should also remember that the recent devaluations of these currencies—15% and 30% respectively—have not, however, managed to revive their domestic economies."

"I think there is even less a probability of a sudden huge devaluation of the yuan because, when the Chinese leaders look at Europe, they only have respect for two countries: Germany and Switzerland. These two are the only ones who have been able to maintain world leadership in highly-coveted industrial niche markets; and, oddly enough, they are the only two countries that have never devalued their currency. I remember, when I was young, one Swiss franc was worth one French franc. Today, it's worth one euro. In the space of a single generation, there has been a six-fold devaluation—that's the legacy my predecessors have left me! On the other hand, four countries have seen a constant decline in their industries' share of the global market: the UK, Italy, Spain... and ourselves. What they have in common is that they have devalued their currencies by 20% in each decade, sparing their manufacturers from the need to increase productivity by at least 2% a year in order to remain competitive on the world stage. The result is that, in France, jobs in industry account for 11% of employment as against 19% on Germany. The Chinese remain convinced that a strong country must have a strong currency if it wants to promote the emergence of a strong industry over the long term."

"We mustn't forget the other aim behind the convertibility of the Chinese currency: to promote investment abroad. This will speed up considerably, particularly in fields linked to technology. Yet another homage to Deng Xiaoping. When he returned to power, having been recalled by Mao at the end of the Cultural Revolution, he was the only Chinese leader at the time to travel abroad, where he discovered the huge gap that separated China from the rest of the world. To fill this gap, foreign investment had to be called on, just as today it is needed to speed up increases in productivity. And this is the way to reach the third objective: a well-supervised diversification of the highest amount of savings in the world. There is no better evidence for this than that supplied by Charles Li, President of the Hong Kong Stock Exchange, who said during a lecture to world investors: 'My last twenty years have been easy in fact: I was the main entry door for capital that wanted to finance the most entrepreneurial blood in the world, that of the Chinese Mainland. The next twenty years will be much more difficult. The challenge will be to find opportunities throughout the world for the diversification of savings accumulated in China. This time, I will be in competition with the whole of the planet!'"

The investor who fell to earth

The President turns to his economic adviser: "Édouard, make a note of all that, will you, and fix up and interview in Paris between Charles Li and Pierre Gattaz of the MEDEF [the largest French employers' federation]. *Have the MEDEF find a way of directing a good part of this windfall capital towards France. Gattaz already has some points to his credit, since, when he was on a trip to Beijing in November 2016, he said: 'I've left a communist country— France—to visit a liberal country—China!'"*

"You can't have forgotten that 1975 film by Jean Yanne—a little masterpiece—called *Les Chinois à Paris* [*The Chinese in Paris*], which portrayed the occupation of Paris by the Chinese army who had set up their headquarters at the Galeries Lafayette department store. Perhaps I should encourage my advisers to see it again ... On a more serious note, I see that Chinese investment abroad is beginning to cause concern, particularly in the USA and in Europe. Recently I was reading a study carried out by a Berlin think-tank which shows that, in 2016, direct investment by China in EU countries increased by 76% to reach 35 billion euros, whilst, on the other hand, investment by European companies in China is stagnating and only amounted to 7 billion euros last year. Even our Germany friends, despite their strong commitment to trade with China, saw some of their politicians get into a sudden panic when the Chinese Midea group bought up the German robotics leader Kuka ..."

"Mr. President, I am convinced that the mergers and acquisitions market is entering a new phase, driven by China. Its foreign investments have to be analysed not only in volume but also qualitatively. We are just at the beginning of a phenomenon which is bound to amplify. It is not just a passing phase, as has been seen in the past at the peak of an economic cycle—as with the Japanese in the late 1980s or in the American private equity funds in 2007. During the first decade of this century, China devoted a measly 2 billion US dollars a year to making direct investments in European companies. This quickly increased to 10 billion in 2010, 20 billion in 2014 and, as you said, 35 billion last year."

"That said, even if Chinese investments sometimes trigger emotional reactions in France, according to my information, accumulated investment remains at a modest level—about 7 billion euros all told—which only amounts to 2% of all foreign investment ..."

"True. And as you pointed out, at the same time, Western investment in China has remained relatively restrained; the USA and Europe each limiting themselves to 8% of a total that is largely in the hands of the Chinese diaspora, principally settled in Asia. But, since 2015, the pace of capital flow has been reaching new levels: now China is investing almost 200 billion US dollars a year in foreign companies and has taken control of European groups such as Pirelli in Italy (for 7 billion euros), the German companies KraussMaffei, EEW Energy and Kuka—the robotics company you mentioned (for 1, 1.4 and 4.5 billion euros respectively), and Syngenta in Switzerland (for 43 billion US dollars). China accounted for almost half of foreign acquisitions in Germany in early 2016, before the German government suddenly tightened things up—a point that hasn't escaped you. The new Chinese owners benefit from financing in the form of almost unlimited loans, as long as their activities comply with the strategic objectives of the Chinese government. Thus ChemChina is able to keep getting into debt, despite a leverage ratio which is unthinkable in the West, by which the amount of its debt reaches nine times its operating cash flow. Furthermore, the heads of the State Grid Corporation, which controls the country's national grid and is about to invest the astronomical sum of 350 billion US dollars over the next five years, have publicly stated that: 'Money is not a problem where foreign acquisitions are concerned.'"

"If I understand you correctly, the huge flow of Chinese funds transformed into American Treasury bonds throughout the first decade of this century will henceforward be invested in taking control of Western companies. To some degree, we should be delighted with this new source of corporate funding, particularly if it enables them to develop. The managers of the Société du Louvre told me recently in private that they are delighted to be able to carry out an ambitious development plan at long last, notably with the setting up of 250 Campanile hotels in China over a three-year period, thanks to their new owner, the Jin Jiang group from Shanghai, after many lean years under the previous shareholders, the Taittinger family. French lifestyle is on to a winner here!"

"I quite agree with you. Ren Jianxin, the President of ChemChina and one of the most aggressive Chinese players in Europe in terms of acquisitions, takes pride in using his limited knowledge of the European business environment when it comes to his integration strategy, thereby leaving the greatest possible freedom to the managers of the companies he targets: 'I am the boss, you are the teacher.'"

"But should we let the Chinese do what they want in Europe without reacting in any way?"

"Of course not, Mr. President! But first of all we should realize how cleverly this investment is being carried out. The specificity of the Chinese approach can clearly be seen in the mega-acquisition of the Swiss agrochemical company, Syngenta—the biggest operation ever undertaken by a Chinese company outside its borders. In 2008, for the first time, China became a net importer of cereals. Panic time! The government attempted to set this situation to rights and identified genetic modification as the solution, concluding in 2013 that this was not a threat to human health. In the past, Chinese leaders had come up against two constraints: firstly, yield from cereals, on average five tonnes per hectare, only reached half the American level; and, secondly, more than 90% of Chinese people said they had no confidence in genetically modified products. ChemChina waited patiently for the right moment before they came out of the woodwork, and did so after Monsanto's failed attempt to take over Syngenta—which somewhat destabilized the heads of the Swiss company. What was new about the Chinese group's approach was to link its offer to the opening up of a huge Chinese market for Syngenta. The Swiss couldn't pass up the chance of such an Eldorado! Once their agreement had been obtained, a hundred or so scientists from the world over, all Nobel prizewinners, signed a petition in the spring of 2016 asking Greenpeace to end its anti-GM campaign because it was not based on any recognised scientific evidence. This was enough to reassure Chinese people that GMOs with the 'Made in Switzerland' label were innocuous. In these circumstances, it was then easy for a state-owned company like ChemChina to obtain the authorisation from the central organization that supervises all the public holdings, the State-Owned Assets Supervision and Administration Commission, abbreviated to SASAC."

The President turns to his advisers: "In the past, De Gaulle used the SAC [the Civic Action Service, a Gaullist militia] to finance things, now it's the Chinese with their SASAC. The world changes but some things never change, do they?"

"I can see that it's a clever strategy, but what you're telling me worries me slightly. If the public coffers are flung wide open to finance foreign acquisitions, even to the extent of the amount you mentioned for Syngenta, doesn't that mean that all large European companies are potential targets for state-owned groups in China, no matter how much capital has to be put in?"

"Don't you believe it, Mr. President. The SASAC doesn't give out money willy-nilly. In fact, it is extremely difficult to persuade a great many of the old guard in China that the country's savings should be spent on enriching foreigners. Wu Xiaohui, who is married to Deng Xiaoping's grand-daughter and is President of the Anbang insurance company, found this out to his own cost when he wanted to buy up the luxury American hotel chain Starwood for the incredible sum of 14 billion US dollars. Over only a few years, his company had managed to pull in almost 20 billion US dollars in annual insurance premiums with which he intended to buy up the jewels of the world luxury hotel industry. He succeeded in acquiring the legendary Waldorf-Astoria in New York for the astronomical sum of more than 2 million US dollars per room. But when it came to Starwood, he was suddenly deprived of financing because of the acquisition price, thought to be unreasonable by the old Chinese *caciques*."

"To sum up: if one plays the game by Chinese rules, investment decisions are more in the hands of the state than in those of company bosses. That means that I too am going to have to behave like a merchant banker with them ... But how can one fight on an equal footing if foreign companies are not welcome in China?"

"You are quite right to underline this point, Mr. President. There are numerous examples showing that China remains very selective when it comes to choosing foreign investors. Sometimes they are excluded out of hand, as in the case of the Western IT industry. After Edward Snowden's revelations, Hewlett-Packard was 'invited' to pass on its server and data storage operations to Tsinghua Unigroup for 2.3 billion US dollars; Cisco, SAP and T-Mobile were obliged to create joint ventures in their respective domains of servers, cloud computing and connected cars, with local partners getting a 51% holding. In the autumn of 2015, IBM even resigned itself to passing all its source codes for services sold in China to the Ministry of Information. Had it not done so, it would have seen itself cut off from access to the most promising information technology market in the world. And it now had to have its research teams remodel products twice yearly, as a defence against any future Chinese copies ..."

"This is all grist to the mill for my argument. Methods of financing and political intervention totally change the rules of the investment game, including in terms of valuation. But I am not convinced that, at the present state of affairs, Europe has the means to resist all that, although, if I understand you well, it is a choice target for Chinese companies ..."

"I believe that, up until the middle of the first decade of this century, the Chinese hoped they could count on Europe to provide a counterweight to American domination. But two major events put a spoke in the wheel of this strategy. First of all, in 2004, Eurostat informed the Council of Europe that statistics coming out of Greece were totally misleading. The only credible defense for the Greeks was to argue that France and Germany were also covering up the extent of their deficits, so that President Chirac and Chancellor Schröder agreed on a general *omerta* at the time. When this came to the ears of the Chinese, it convinced them that Europe was not a 'well-run household.' Then, in 2005, the French and Dutch no-votes during the referendums on a European Constitution killed off any remaining illusions the Chinese might have had about a European edifice being able to rival the USA. From that time on, Chinese strategy changed. It now consists in acting opportunistically: either a country-by-country approach, by playing on rivalries within the Union and exploiting each member's weaknesses; or, when it is more favorable to China to do so, a pan-European approach to counter any country putting up resistance."

"What you're saying is sending shivers up my spine. I am well aware that the first project of my mandate will be to try and rebuild the Franco-German relationship. Today, it is as if our two countries were separated *de facto*. Germany only needs France in order to cover up the extent of its strength, and France uses Germany in order to hide the extent of its weakness. My concern—which I believe is shared by the Chinese elite—is that Germany, whilst remaining quite naturally moored to Europe, might leave the euro. While Greece showed that it was not politically possible to leave from the basement, I fear that Germany may prove that it may be economically desirable to leave from the ceiling. Germany has been keenly observing how a country like Switzerland has adapted to the sudden appreciation of its currency—which has increased in value by a staggering 60% with regard to the Euro in only eight years since the 2008 financial crisis. If Germany has welcomed in a million immigrants, this is because, in the long term, they are destined to carry out the tasks with low added value, tasks which would become non-competitive in case of a sudden re-evaluation. Therefore, I have the feeling that the Germans, under the impressive leadership of Wolfgang Schäuble, are preparing themselves in case I should fail in my attempt to reform the country radically. China would emerge as the big winner, with its main foreign market—Europe—incapable of defending its interests collectively. Brexit can only bolster China in its divide and conquer approach, since it is convinced that, in fact, it will be the main beneficiary. I have also noted that, only a few weeks after the British vote, the first issue of the European edition of China's propaganda medium, *Global Times*, sported the headline '*You exit, We enter!*'"

"They couldn't be any clearer way to say that Chinese are continuing to go shopping in Europe—like the 14% stake acquired at a huge discount in PSA in France, or the acquisition of the airport in Ciudad Real, a city of 75,000 inhabitants 200 kilometres south of Madrid, for only ... the symbolic sum of 10,000 euros! The Spanish state had spent almost a billion euros on a facility with a four-kilometre runway designed to take the Airbus A380 and which could handle ten million passengers a year! In the same way, thanks to its dumping strategy, China has appropriated almost the whole solar energy manufacturing sector. It is preparing to repeat the maneuver in the semi-conductor industry; rumor has it that the extravagant sum of 100 billion US dollars has been put at the disposal of Tsinghua Unigroup to finance its shopping in this domain. It's enough to give sleepless nights to the bosses of these former- jewels in the crown of Europe, like STMicroelectronics, erstwhile leader of this key sector. Its turnover decreased by 22% between 2005 and 2015, thanks to—if one can say that—a Franco-Italian state co-governance which looks like putting the company in the obituary column."

"Are you then among those who fear the famous 'Chinese invasion,' so dear to the heart of Jean Yanne?"

"No, Mr. President. My conclusion is rather that, in a multipolar world, China is going to regain its rightful place. Looking at it over the long term, it is its disappearance from the world stage for more than a century that was an anomaly of history."

SHOP UNTIL THEY DROP

"Since we're now on to the cheese course, my dear friend, may I suggest we accompany it with a Côte-Rôtie—the favorite wine of Louis XIV. And we must be prepared to toast our Chinese friends and their recent but passionate conversion to our great French wines, the perfect symbol of their new consumer society. People are always going on about this new Chinese middle class with their apparently insatiable appetite. But if that were the case, our exports should be benefiting far more, and yet we keep having an extremely large trade deficit. Does this mean that this thirst for consumption has been overestimated or that one billion three hundred million Chinese, whose expenditure on consumer goods only accounts for 35% of GDP, are buying mostly Chinese products?"

"Mr. President, we first have to understand the singular nature of the Chinese consumer that I see every day, realize the limits of the emergence of a true middle class, and comprehend to what extent the notion of productivity will be a determining factor in the future development of consumption. You know the old French adage: 'History never serves up the same dish twice.'[1] It is even more compelling when the dish has never been served up in the first place. In China, the generation now in power had no 'dishes' to feed itself on during the Cultural Revolution, which lasted close to ten years, up until the early 1970s. Yan Lan, the perfect example of the Princeling 'club,' is a brilliant Chinese woman who opened the Beijing offices of the Gide law firm and then of the Lazard bank. She recently told *Le Point* magazine of the impact of these painful memories, which are still well present today: 'I always have the impression of lagging behind, of

---

1   The equivalent of 'History never repeats itself.'

trying to catch up for that lost decade. It has taught me to face up to problems and has given me an optimistic outlook.' This is echoed in the words of a Chinese woman friend of mine. When I asked her which of the two cities she had lived in—Shanghai or Beijing—she preferred, she said: 'Shanghai, of course! Because the places you go to when you go out are closer together. You can even go to two different parties in one evening!' This need to make up for the time lost by previous generations is for me one of the essential elements that explain the speed with which the Chinese have entered the digital world. Add to this the one-child policy and you get a consumer with a unique behavior pattern—a person who is 'not like us.' First of all, he or she is young, whilst in the West, money is in the hands of older people. A Chinese investor who specializes in the consumer goods sector told me his best kept secret one day: 'I only talk to people born after 1985. Firstly, because they are the result of the one-child policy. Secondly, because they are the children of the Internet generation. In 2000, China had only four million Internet users, so someone who was over 15 at the time is not a digital native. And in China, it is the young who benefit from their parents' and grandparents' savings.' So, in China, the average age of someone buying a new car is 36, whereas it is 46 in the USA and 56 in Germany. It is therefore logical for specialists in the sector to count on the market for connected vehicles taking off much faster in China than in the rest of the world. We have to understand the motivations of this new Chinese youth if we want to cater to its aspirations."

"My dear chap, if I only addressed myself to French people born after 1985, I wouldn't get many votes ... But I see what you mean about the importance of understanding this new generation. Recently I met the President of AccorHotels, Sébastien Bazin, who told me he had created a shadow Board of Directors comprising six young men and seven young women aged 25, whom he asks for an opinion on major decisions being made. According to him, it is the best way of keeping in touch with new consumers in the hotel sector. Maybe I should create my own Shadow Cabinet with ten or so young people, to help me run France? It would certainly be more effective than the Wednesday cabinet meetings ..."

"My limited experience of the board meetings of a start-up has taught me that a board should only have three, five or seven members, never more, if you want to have productive meetings. But, getting back to our subject: young means fickle. 75% of Chinese buying new cars say they intend to buy a different make next time. The explosion of selfies has revolutionized behavior patterns when it comes to buying clothes: in each photo—now taken daily—you have to be wearing something different. Hence the success of Zara and H&M with their ranges of accessories at unbeatable prices, whilst their competitor American Apparel, which was locked into its classic model of seasonal—and expensive—collections, has gone bankrupt. Young also means easy to influence: two-thirds of purchases made online are the result of word-of-mouth from friends or family, as against only a third in the USA. It is true to say that, in China, tradition has it that you follow the winner—like casino gamblers who follow in the tracks of the evening's lucky winner. Young means fast and technologically savvy: 500 million smartphones have been sold in only two years, i.e. a penetration level of almost 100% of the urban market, whilst the uptake on high-tech products in the West takes nearer four to six years, going from geeks and early adopters to mainstream users and finally latecomers ... E-commerce is in full swing, already accounting for 14% of retail sales and 50% of world digital commerce. The social media site WeChat had the ingenious idea of digitalizing the red envelopes in which cards and cash gifts are distributed on Chinese New Year. In 2016, 32 billion cards were exchanged in only a few days. It has to be said that WeChat developed a special application for the occasion: selfies sent to friends and family remained blurred if the recipient didn't send back a gift envelope with a substantial sum inside it ..."

"Are you suggesting that if I want to give my family some foie gras for Christmas, I should only do so if I get back an envelope with some hard cash in it? People like you will turn Santa Claus into a nasty old money-grabber."

"That reminds me of what a Chinese woman friend once said to me: 'You Westerners are incapable of doing business within the family. Why do you think we get together at the New Year? It's for business.' Everyone has to show how creative they are, like the online travel agency Ctrip which has created a virtual tour operator. All of its clients who are going to the same destination on the same date are brought together in ephemeral communities so that they can share their experiences online and in real time ... Young also means insatiable and with a thirst for knowledge: according to the recruiting firm Michael Page, 67% of salaried staff in Hong Kong plan to change jobs during the subsequent twelve months. A Chinese tourist who spends five days on the island of Phuket in Thailand will stay in five different hotels. The idea of packing and unpacking suitcases may well horrify us but the Chinese get enormous pleasure out of taking photos in each hotel which they will show off to their friends when they get back in order to impress them. The bosses of the Club Méditerranée which offers winter sports holidays near Beijing didn't expect their clients to say, after only half a day of a week's stay: 'Skiing's great! Done that! Now what's the afternoon activity?' In fact, the Chinese only spend an average of three days at the Club, instead of the usual seven days for Westerners."

"We should offer them five days in Paris with a Ritz-Plaza-Meurice-George V- Raphaël package deal. They could even hunt for Pokemons on the way ..."

"Young means large numbers. The Chinese market is a wonderful opportunity for anyone who wants to seize it: the Causeway Bay Apple Store in Hong Kong, the largest in the world, brings in 1 billion US dollars in annual turnover on its own; according to the most reputable analysts of the automobile industry, BMW and Volkswagen get between a third and half of their global profits—depending on the year—from China; at the present time, as many 4G phones are being sold in China as in Europe and the USA combined; every day, 9,000 Chinese get on a plane for the first time! Such a critical mass should have a real impact in the future on product design and product standards. Finally, young means 'not like us': you can expect to see our beaches invaded... but only in the evening when the sun has set; and to have our restaurants furnished with large round tables so that grannies won't get neckache from turning to look at their only grandson during family banquets ...."

"I will willingly admit that the Chinese consumer is one of a kind. But, like any other human being, he or she also appreciates the major international brands, and seems to me just as susceptible to the good old recipe of the Roman Empire, *panem et circenses*—bread and games. I see too that the Chinese are also coming to Europe looking for agricultural land and football clubs ...."

"Quite right, Mr. President. But, these days, if the older generation in China knew Latin as well as you do, it would undoubtedly exclaim '*O tempora, O mores.*' In fact, a recent study by the McKinsey strategy consultancy pointed out that, for the first time, there is a fundamental change coming about in the behavior pattern of young Chinese people: they now say they prioritize happiness over wealth. This reflects the fact that young people are disappointed that they haven't been able to acquire wealth as easily as their elders with the real estate bubble, but also shows a quest for new values and new experiences. A new shift has also come to light recently: in sectors as diverse as cars, cosmetics and food, the year 2015 marked a gradual return to Chinese brands."

"I had the pleasure of meeting our compatriot Catherine Becker who, in her book *La Marque rouge*,[2] gives an excellent account of how, from the 1980s onwards, Deng Xiaoping was initially very welcoming to Western brands. Deng was worried by the social instability of the post-Mao era and saw these brands as the embodiment of a superior order that was as respected by the Western population as Maoism had been in its time. He thought that importing the thirst for consumer goods from the West was a good way of channeling the new energies that had been let loose in his country."

"Today we're in almost the opposite situation. The Hong Kong department store Lane Crawford already stocks the brands of thirty talented young Chinese designers, as opposed to only four brands three years ago. Even in the field of cosmetics, nine Chinese brands figure among the first ten on the online trading site Tmall. This is all the more significant in a country where confidence is transmitted directly between Internet users, which makes brand management and follow-up even more difficult than it is in the West."

"We politicians are also faced with the danger of the rise of the social media which challenge our opinion pollsters—who still work on traditional models. We're living in unprecedented times when confidence is moving from the institution to the individual. You've mentioned commercial brands in this respect, but it is also true for information—every blogger imagines he or she is a journalist—and even for politics with every chairperson of a charity dreaming of being a government minister!"

---

2   The Red Brand

"It's notably the power of word-of-mouth in China that explains why Chinese consumers, whenever they can, are turning more and more to national brands, encouraged by government propaganda which, with regard to foreign brands, is re-using the wonderful slogan used for the launch of the Fiat Uno in France: 'Y'a moins bien, mais c'est plus cher!'[3] Go and visit a Hong Kong merchant banker: if he is Western, he will try and sell you Western brands about to conquer Asia; if he is Asian, he will only propose local brands as future market winners, like the giant Kweichow moutai which has become the second leading global brand in the spirits sector!"

"Your analysis seems to presage a rather less rosy future in China for our major international brands than I thought. But, logically speaking, the rise of the middle class and the increase in its purchasing power should push it towards quality and therefore towards Western products ..."

A middle class lost in the middle?

"You're touching on a highly sensitive subject, Mr. President—one that all the heads of major foreign consumer goods groups in China are working on. How big really is this middle-class? Consultancy firms put a high estimate on it, suggesting a market of 200 to 300 million people. Other experts, like the Gavkal Dragonomics teams in Hong Kong under the guidance of Arthur Kroeber, base themselves on the Western criterion of an annual income of 25,000 US dollars and estimate the market at around 100 million, a figure that could double in five to ten years' time. Intuitively, I would say that this estimate seems more reasonable, particularly if you take other data into account: about 80 million foreign cars; 45 million children having private lessons, costing

---

3   'You'll find lower quality, but it'll be more expensive!'

300 US dollars a month; 80 million Chinese tourists goingING abroad 1.5 times a year on average; and 70 million iPhones sold by Apple in two years. Similarly, HSBC experts estimate the luxury market at about 10 million customers, and the lifestyle market at 80 million. These figures are confirmed by analyses carried out the by Club Méditerranée, which evaluates their potential market at 75 million Chinese 'gentils membres.'"[4]

"So it's less than 10% of the population. But we're still talking about one or two hundred million individuals, whose income will increase in years to come ... It's one of the foremost consumer markets in the world, and I don't see on what basis our major groups can ignore such a potential goldmine ..."

"From a macro-economic point of view, you are quite right. But there is one obstacle: the inequality of the distribution of wealth in China. We are not dealing with a socially homogenous group—far from it. The Chinese middle class is not going to develop along the lines of the Japanese or the Koreans in the second half of the 20th century. Chinese society is anything but 'harmonious,' in contradiction with the official slogan of government leaders under the previous President, Hu Jintao. Bear in mind that almost 200 million migrants from rural areas are still living in cities without a residence permit—a *hukuo*—a fact which deprives them of any safety net provided by social welfare. They account for a third of the urban population, and up to half of those living in cities like Shanghai or Beijing."

"Rather as if half of Parisians were illegal immigrants! Hardly imaginable in France where we don't really like homeless people."

"And the real risk is that the inequality gap will widen rather than be reduced, particularly if the future means increased automation in China. The highly-reputable Boston Consulting

---

4 "nice guests"

Group estimates that 85% of growth in Chinese consumption over the next ten years will come from the most well-to-do group—those with incomes over 25,000 US dollars a year. On the other hand, in the less well-off Tier III and Tier IV cities, the future looks much less rosy. This is something that the biggest Chinese property developer Dalian Wanda has already alluded to by withdrawing from the residential and commercial markets of these localities. He is now focusing on the largest metabolizes and only on commercial premises."

"And yet I have the impression that the subject of inequality— which goes deeper than we might think—remains largely taboo for the authorities. I have taken care not to mention this in my exchanges with Beijing, probably inspired by an enlightening local proverb: 'Give a horse to the man who tells the truth, he will need it to make his escape!' But, listening to you, it seems we have to expect a future slowdown in domestic consumption, and yet the government's watchword is to rely on this middle class and its thirst for buying things to get the economy back on an even keel. Aren't you being a bit pessimistic?"

"I don't think so, Mr. President. I am convinced that, in fact, the more the Chinese government makes official denials about the growing imbalances in the country, the more the problem of the slowdown in domestic consumption will become more obvious as time goes by."

"That reminds me again of Winston Churchill who said, 'Never believe any information unless it has been officially denied at least five times!'"

"Without wanting to throw too many figures at you—the briefing notes from your advisers must be stuffed full of them—but I think it may be useful to point out that, for 2016, growth in disposable income has been estimated at only 6% or 7%, which shows that the declared objective of 10% cannot be maintained. In 2015, the consumer goods market decreased in volume by 1%, its 3% increase in value being due only to a mix effect of rising prices. For example, the beer and instant noodle markets—the typical meal of the poorest class—suffered a significant drop in volume. In December 2015, for the first time, the level of confidence in future income development, published by the Central Bank, sank to below 50%. In early 2016, net migration from the country to the cities was negative for the first time in decades. Guangdong province announced a wage freeze for two years, in contradiction with the national five-year plan's objective of doubling income within a decade."

"I see you're joining the camp of those who foresee a somewhat hard landing of the Chinese economy. This worries me a great deal, particularly because, since 2008, it has been China that has fuelled between a third and half of world growth—depending on the year in question."

"Don't worry, the slowdown of Chinese growth has already taken place. When you're an investor, you always think in terms of value and not growth, and take monetary developments into account. Only two or three years ago, the country was growing by almost 10% in volume, whilst the currency was appreciating by 5% compared to a basket of comparable currencies, i.e. a growth in value of about 15%. Today, the 6% to 7% growth announced by the government, real though it may be, is lessened by the 5% to 6% devaluation of the Chinese currency, which means that the growth in value is in fact minimal ..."

"I agree with you about growth in China. Slowdown has happened. However, the Chinese government has been extremely clever in seeking to farm out the consequences, particularly to countries producing raw materials: in 2015, their exports decreased by almost 450 billion US dollars, an amount equivalent to the trade surplus of that same year! This looks strangely like a suction effect of the same level as the monetary easing carried out in Europe by the ECB to the tune of 1,000 billion euros over two years. With the huge advantage of not suddenly depreciating the Chinese currency by 20%, which was what the euro suffered without even triggering any durable economic recovery. For us Europeans, there is a lesson to be learned there as far as the future is concerned."

"The Chinese government is perfectly aware of this slowdown. That's why, as soon as it happened in 2012, the government quite rightly pronounced the diagnosis that the future was in reviving productivity in China."

Productivity does strike twice

"Productivity. You've said the word. You explained a few minutes ago that capital productivity in certain sectors like finance has undergone a spectacular rise—thanks to the inrush of new technology of course, but above all because of new private players. However, the economic counselor at our Beijing embassy has come to the conclusion that labor productivity in the large state-owned enterprises in the industrial sector is a major source of concern ..."

"Unlike lightning, Mr. President, productivity is going to strike twice! The nature of growth in China is going to evolve: in the past it has meant mobilizing the country's vast resources, but now it means facing up to the challenge of optimizing their use."

"So, after perspiration, inspiration! That augurs a rather happier picture of prospects in the future."

"These days, labor productivity in China is estimated to be a fifth of the USA level. However, according to the experts of Oxford

Economics, unit labor costs are only 4% lower than the American level, which partly explains the industrial relocation beginning in the USA. As long as low wages were kept within the range of 50 to 100 US dollars a month, the question of labor costs didn't come into play. But Chinese salaried staff have just gone through a decade when their pay rates have soared. In Guangdong province, for example, in the south of the country—the famous 'world's factory' which employs nearly 200 million workers—wages are now reaching 400 to 500 US dollars a month. Of course, the improvement in the lot of Chinese workers is good news. But the consequences in terms of productivity are not such good news: the unit labor cost has soared, particularly in low value-added sectors like the textile industry, which has had to relocate to neighboring countries like Vietnam, Cambodia or Burma; even to Africa—to Ethiopia, for example."

"Generally speaking, there is only one solution to this problem: go upmarket, improve the technological content of products, even import from abroad and automate production. That's what the Chinese government is trying to do at the moment ..."

"Quite so, Mr. President. I would even go so far as to say that this is what it has constantly been doing ever since the launch of economic reforms. As in the steel industry, which is a subject of fierce debate between China and Europe at the present time. Even before 1978, when Deng Xiaoping was recalled to power by Mao, he had noted that Chinese steel production—around 20 million tonnes—was insufficient, and that it was necessary to open China up to foreign groups. It was only when he returned to lead the country after Mao died that he was able to put this strategy into effect. One of his first initiatives in 1978–1979 was even to go to Singapore, where he was surprised by the success achieved by the leaders of Chinese origin of this island state. Lee Kuan Yew explained to Deng that the secret of the 'dragon city' lay in having compensated for its lack of raw materials by opening up to foreign capital and talent as far back as the early days of independence. Deng then went to Japan, the USA and Europe. After that, he never left China again until his death, but this did not prevent him from getting the most out of the lessons learned from his few trips abroad."

"I'm not thinking along the same lines as you. An approach that depends mostly on importing foreign technology has its limits. Even in the West, cultural barriers hinder cooperation between countries. In Europe, the success of Airbus is an exception, for numerous attempts to import American technology here have proved difficult to set up."

"I'm with you with regard to cultural differences between the West and China. For one thing, there's the language barrier. Only a few people speak English. Your official schedule will unfortunately deprive you of the pleasure of asking a Beijing taxi driver, in English, to take you to 'Tiananmen Square.' You'll find out that, in comparison, a Paris taxi driver seems almost friendly! Lee Kuan Yew, in a series of interviews published during the last years of his life in *The Grand Master's Insights on China, the United States and the World,* pointed out that one of the criteria for the successful development of China in the future would be how quickly the use of English could spread, particularly for attracting the best brains in the world, something that was so beneficial to the USA in the 20th century. But there is a long way to go before large numbers of foreign students do doctoral courses at the universities of Tsinghua in Beijing or Fudan in Shanghai, whereas, in the USA, foreigners—often from Asia—make up about half the numbers of students at that level. Contrary to what one might think in this era of technology and artificial intelligence, the language factor plays an important role, since Westerners find it difficult to master the language of Confucius. It takes 12,000 hours of teaching to become in any way fluent."

"Language has always been a huge barrier to getting anywhere in China, even in the time of the mandarins who saw the written language as a way of keeping the people well away from the running of the Empire."

"It is my belief, Mr. President, that in the quest for improved productivity, Chinese culture will play an important part, particularly in the booming service sector. I experienced this directly when I was teaching in Beijing. I would ask my students regularly if they had any questions to ask, but no hand was ever raised in public. I finally realized that this apparent timidity came from their cultural tradition which requires that, in a Chinese classroom, the teacher speaks and the students listen. They must at no time interrupt the smooth running of the lesson. So I suggested we had a ten-minute break every hour during which time they would get together in groups of four and then a designated spokesperson for each group would ask a question in front of the class. In a fraction of a second, the religious silence that reigned in the classroom changed into a hubbub worthy of the noisiest fish market—a sign of the wonderful ebullience of modern youth once it has been unfettered!"

"That remark reminds me of an exchange I had with the American manager of a large hotel in Beijing. I asked him about the greatest challenge that was facing him, and he said that he had to employ on average two people to do the work of one Westerner. As long as pay remained low, this had been manageable, but wage inflation was now posing a considerable threat to its profitability. The main source of the problem, according to him, was delegation of responsibility. In a service industry like the hotel business, and unlike manufacturing industry, each employee is called on to take personal initiatives—even to a minimal degree—on a daily basis, to cater to guests' unexpected needs. As heirs to a management culture in which the stick was used far more often than the carrot, Chinese employees always live in fear of making a mistake if they don't follow a procedure that has been clearly laid down and learned. They therefore prefer not to take any initiatives rather than run the risk of doing something wrong. What the hotel manager did therefore was to affect two employees to each post where contact with the guests was involved. Each one was therefore freed from direct responsibility for, if a mistake were to be made, it would be impossible to determine which of the two was really to blame. But this is a highly inefficient system and reminds me of what Pope Pius VI said when someone asked him how many people worked in the Vatican: 'About half of them!' Soviet workers summed up the productivity question in this phrase: 'They pretend to pay us, we pretend to work.' But I don't think the Soviet model turned out to be a model of remarkable economic efficiency, any more than the Russian model today."

"Except perhaps for Xi Jinping, who is apparently fascinated by the fact that after twenty years of autocratic power, Vladimir Putin's popularity in Russia is still at record levels—and he has always been democratically elected ... But, thankfully, China has other models in mind apart from the Russian one when it comes to addressing the problem of productivity. The authorities know that they are immersed in a vicious cycle: balancing the economy by counting on domestic consumption means that purchasing power, and therefore salaries, continue to increase, and that this rise in payroll costs can only be absorbed if there is a rise in labor productivity. This is now a national priority."

"That does not seem to me to be out of their reach. After all, the potential for improvement, particularly in comparison with the USA, is very high. It is nothing like the situation in Europe, for example, where each extra point gained in productivity is only won by considerable effort. Just look at the battle engaged between France and Germany on this issue ..."

"Quite so, Mr. President. And besides, leaders as well as numerous economists recognize that productivity in the West has been at a standstill for many years, in spite of the effects of the digital revolution. Even in Singapore, which is the star pupil, productivity has not increased since 2011. We are also seeing major European groups—including those performing best on the CAC40—having trouble making any significant progress in generating internal innovation. This is a phenomenon that the large pharmaceutical groups have been experiencing for a long time and is now spreading to other sectors, like that of everyday consumer goods. For shareholders, this inability has serious consequences, if we are to judge by the disquieting rise in the amounts that are being paid to acquire the creative talents in start-ups. It is no longer uncommon to see companies pay from four to six times the annual turnover of their targets: Danone paid 12.5 billion US dollars for WhiteWave Foods (four times its revenue) in order to catch up with the organic trend in the USA; L'Oréal paid 1.2 billion US dollars for IT Cosmetics (six times its revenue) in order to acquire new know-how in dermatology; and Unilever paid 1 billion US dollars for Shaving Club—a company that did not exist five years ago—in order to get into the segment of shaving products for men."

"What you're saying is that, to a certain degree, the big Western groups are being confronted with the same problem as their Chinese counterparts: the lack of innovation. In our case, the origin of this is in a refusal to pay the right price for creative talent; in the Chinese case, it's because of a lack of employee training. And all this at a time when everything is on the move, as Jean-Paul Agon, President of L'Oréal, told me recently: 'Our environment has changed more in the last three years than in all my thirty-five years at L'Oréal.'"

"Remember, Mr. President, the crucial importance of timing. It could be lucky for China that it has to obtain productivity increases just at the moment when, thanks to the digital revolution, productivity will probably skyrocket once again. This is not yet visible since the first phase of this revolution mostly involved individuals who saw their lives change radically, notably because of the social media. It is my belief that the second stage will essentially involve the business world."

"For the moment, it's true that in the minds of the general public, the digital economy has mostly produced entertainment for consumers and jobs for the lesser-qualified, like drivers for e-commerce deliveries or for Uber."

"Digitalization has mainly affected tasks in marketing and distribution. In the mobile phone sector, for example, the cost of acquiring a new customer was about 300 euros twenty years ago, whereas, nowadays, an efficiently-managed advertising campaign on Facebook has brought this down to 30 euros—a tenfold increase in productivity! But other jobs in companies have not yet benefited from this revolution. That's where China means to surprise us in the years to come."

THE WAKE-UP CALL

"Let me try and sum up what we're talking about here. First of all, from where we are sitting, our vision of China is largely distorted. We hold somewhat extreme opinions although China's world is highly complex and is constantly evolving. This leads us either to seriously overestimate or underestimate its capacities, according to whether one is a 'sino-fan or a sino-sceptic.' From my point of view, I believe that its leaders have the deep conviction that they are making a new leap forward in economic reform, perhaps as big as the one achieved by Deng Xiaoping. I also believe that we must not forget the difficulties facing them, given what you have said about the state of Chinese society and the imbalances which continue to undermine it. Xi Jinping wants to reclaim all the grandeur of the Empire. So well and good. But there is the rest of the world as well. Generally speaking, I tend to like surprises, but I am rather wary of surprises coming from our Chinese friends. So I am wondering what surprises they have in store for us in the future."

"Mr. President, my analysis is that we shall be getting both a nice and a nasty surprise. Let's start by the nasty one. The so-called new development model, which depends on the growth in domestic consumption will in fact peter out more quickly than predicted: it will level out well below the 15% required to put the system firmly back on an even keel. We've already talked about the reasons for this: salaries not increasing as fast in the future, the end of the real estate bubble, the explosion of pensions that have to be financed. The nice surprise will be that, far from taking refuge in pessimism, China will try to institute a new development drive centered on productivity increases. Just when economists are having doubts about the West's ability to generate new productivity increases, China is going to surprise its doomsayers."

"If I put myself in the shoes of my Chinese counterparts, I would be very hopeful on reading the World Bank's reports forecasting that, in the next ten years, 60% of the one billion people coming on to the world labor market will be doing jobs that don't exist at the moment. In a country that is creating 13 million new jobs a year and cutting 12 million of them, the opportunity to build a new world is not to be missed."

"That's exactly what Bernard Charlès—the President of Dassault Systems and without doubt one of the Frenchmen with the best understanding of the changes to come in the next decade—meant when he said: 'The industrialist's job is not to optimize the present, but to organize new territories properly ... The real power of digitalization is the power of the imagination. We are no longer in a product economy, but an economy of usage and experience ... We must invent a world based on the harmony between products, nature and life ... Industrial value is moving towards a virtual model, in which data may become the main source of energy, as long new experiments in usage can emerge from it ... It is in cloud services that value will be concentrated.'"

"I entirely share that belief. It hasn't escaped me that the leading taxi firm in the world, Uber, does not possess any vehicles; that the leading hotel business, Airbnb owns no hotel rooms; that the leading telephone companies, Skype, WhatsApp and WeChat own no networks; that the leading distributor, Alibaba, has no stock; that the leading social media, Facebook, creates no content; that the leading film distributor, Netflix, has no cinemas; and that the two leading software suppliers, Google and Apple, create no applications ... In the last century, the most creative minds went into the legal field. Remember what Giraudoux wrote in *La Guerre de Troie d'aura pas lieu*:[1] 'Law is the most powerful school of the imagination. No poet has ever interpreted nature more freely than lawyers have interpreted facts.' Nowadays, it's the digital revolution that attracts them—Bernard Charlès being a case in point. That's why I am totally convinced that the success or failure of my mandate will depend solely on our country's ability to adapt to the coming revolutions."

"Mr. President, you will be able to share your revolutionary zeal, since you face the same intellectual barricades as your Chinese contacts. I believe they are totally capable of imposing a new development model—which I would call 'frugal'—on a global scale, and of launching a new 'Great Leap Forward—Season 4.0.' This will give birth to a new China before our very eyes. A new China still trying to-co-exist with the old China."

The "frugal Ferrari"

"You intrigue me ... One China is already complicated enough, but two?"

"Let me tell you a little story. After wining and dining rather well, one of my Shanghai friends found himself on the Bund— the Shanghai equivalent of the Champs-Élysées—at 1 o'clock in the morning. Since he couldn't find a taxi, he used the app for Didi Dache—the Chinese Uber—which told him there was a Ferrari available in the next ten minutes. Thinking it was a hoax, he nevertheless confirmed the order, and it was indeed a Ferrari that arrived. As they were speeding towards the former French concession, they stopped at a red light and my friend began a conversation with the driver:

'Is it worth your while working for Didi like this all day long?'

---

1   *The Trojan War Will Not Take Place*

'I don't know. I'm the CEO of a flourishing e-commerce company. I only take passengers late at night when I'm going home from work.'

'I don't quite understand. You don't seem to need to do it really. So why do you do it?'

'Well, some poor guy has got to pay for the petrol ...'

To my mind, this little anecdote presages the birth of a 'frugal' Chinese business model, which will be the clear winner in the 21st century. In one sense, the coming era presents an incredible opportunity: the number of people with access to the consumer goods market and Internet will go up tenfold. We have grown up among 700 million lucky Westerners—mainly American and European. But our children have the great fortune to be surrounded by seven billion individuals. Thanks to the magic of the Internet, they can contact friends in all corners of the world, and 'flatten out' our globe far beyond our childhood dreams. For an imaginative entrepreneur, this revolution is a unique chance to use the leverage of new technology to conquer the whole world. But there is one thing we must offer in return: to be able to divide today's cost structure by ten. This will be the only way to make a product or a service affordable for the whole of the New World."

"We must have been reading the same things. What you are saying reminds me of a book called *From Zero to One* by Peter Thiel, a German who has settled in California—a book that has pride of place on my desk at the Élysée. In it, Thiel explains how he has always attempted to finance future sustainable monopolies, whose performance is exponentially increased by technology. I believe that he, among others, is one of the founders of PayPal. This interests me particularly because these technological monopolies are new things to be dealt with by governments and pose a whole series of questions, including regulatory ones, which I should like to answer in a way that is both fair and as little penalizing as possible."

"Unlike Westerners, the Chinese are not so interested in invention itself. In China, what counts above all is innovation, to be able to transform a business model by upsetting the value chain or creating a totally new customer experience. Like the frugal Ferrari. They are taking the value chains of all our industries to pieces and, at each stage, ask themselves whether the end user is really ready to pay such a price for the perceived value added. If they identify an imbalance between the service rendered and the price paid, they propose new, lighter and much cheaper solutions. Our Shanghai taxi driver agrees to put money into Ferrari's coffers because his supercar gives him a high social standing. But paying for petrol is a common-or-garden activity with no added value, so why not have that done by an external source? This is a disconcerting approach for Western competitors of new Chinese companies entering the market, in sectors like telephony. The West, meanwhile, is reassured because it sees an absence of invention in China and doesn't see that it is using its imagination to innovate by stripping away superfluous functions from their products. Moreover, if I asked you who invented the car engine, what would your answer be?"

The President calls over his economic adviser: "Édouard, this is the sort of question you were ready to answer at the oral to get into ENA, right?" He looks quizzically at his diplomatic adviser and his communications adviser as well. They both remain silent.

"Right. As usual, I'm the one who has to do the work. I would say a Frenchman or a German in the late 19th century. If I'm wrong, may I remind you, my dear advisers, of George Mandel's words when asked to define his role as Clemenceau's Chief of Staff: 'When he farts, I'm the one who stinks!' You'd better pray that my answer's correct!"

"And if I asked you who made the car into a mass-produced product?"

"That's Henry Ford, of course."

"Have no fear, Mr. President, I am just as ignorant as your advisers. I had to look the subject up on Wikipedia to realize that those who first perfected the combustion engine are mostly unknown, with the exception of Gottlieb Daimler who improved on a concept invented by Alphonse Beau de Rochas in the 1860s. This proves that history is willfully ungrateful to inventors and rewards innovators. China's great strength is that it focuses solely on applied research and its industrial extensions, whist we French continue to prioritize fundamental research. This is the strength of Chinese creativity: in sport, it has never won the most medals at an Olympic Games, but, to this day, Beijing remains the only city in the world to have hosted both the summer and winter Olympics ... That surely deserves the best gold medal of all."

"I am quite willing to believe that the political world is seeing the baton passed in a very similar way as between inventors and innovators. It's not always those who start revolutions who benefit from it afterwards. It's a historical constant, from Versailles in 1789 to Cairo in 2011. Unfortunately, the front runners soon end up coming last. But what strikes me about the emergence of the new frugal way that you mention is its global dimension; it's as if the rest of the world were starting to take inspiration from Chinese successes by following its two main principles: starting from a blank page and maximizing the leverage of the Internet and technology. The blank page has inspired numerous 'disrupters' all over the world and in all fields. A student who could hardly keep body and soul together, created the Soylent company, which invented the 1,500 calorie drink, lowering the price of a meal from 10–15 dollars to only 2.75 dollars. Kenya is reworking its electricity distribution into independent local networks, for a tenth of the cost of national networks constructed in Europe. Rwanda is building the first 'aero-drone' in the world, to deliver emergency pharmaceutical supplies to remote villages with no access by road ..."

"Meanwhile, France has built half of the roundabouts in the world, costing ten times more than traffic lights; and has beaten the world record in motorway construction costs by spending 1 billion 600 million euros on a 13-kilometre motorway on La Réunion—130 million euros a kilometre!"

"I see that, like me, you are an avid reader of the annual report of the National Audit Office—I only wish that, one day, it would become an Amazon best-seller in France!"

"The Chinese quest for frugality goes far beyond products that are traditionally cheap. It now extends to the service sector in which China is anticipating a boom in the future. I read somewhere that in the field of healthcare for the elderly, China is far more interested in home care which it wants to be able to provide for less than 500 US dollars a month, whereas, here, being in a retirement home costs between 3,000 and 5,000 euros a month. The Western model would be especially difficult to operate on a large scale in China because real estate magnates don't look favorably on any geographical concentration of dead people, because, according to tradition, they have wandering souls, and this would lower the prices of nearby housing by at least 20% ..."

"You are perfectly right to mention the healthcare sector. Chinese medicine fascinates me: the combination of traditional medicine and Western techniques will, I believe, be the best way of avoiding the inflation in healthcare costs which continues to undermine the West, starting with the USA. The fact that Tu Youyou was the first Chinese woman to be awarded the Nobel Prize for medicine in 2015, is a consecration of her work in this field and can only encourage the country to defy Western arrogance on the subject."

"I would add that, in the art of marketing, creativity is not the preserve of the West alone. The smartphone manufacturer Xiaomi had the idea of replacing costly traditional marketing experts by a team of ten or so newly-qualified graduates. Their first task was to highlight the extreme thinness of the latest model compared to its competitor Apple. They produced a viral video on the Internet in which two friends are having a drink in a bar. One of them takes out his Apple, the other then takes a frying pan and hits the cellphone which changes from an Apple into a super-thin Xiaomi. These highly-gifted young people then launched a massive sales promotion campaign offering the combined purchase of a cellphone and a frying pan ... It was such a success that Xiaomi couldn't get enough frying pans! So say goodbye to the huge marketing budgets that our large Western groups are used to, which, like Nestlé in China, are having trouble reducing their cost base to cater to the needs of a middle class without sufficient means ..."

"That reminds me a little of what Xavier Niel did with Free[2] and what Renault did with the Logan ..."

"Indeed. And the beauty of it all is that it is viral and crosses all frontiers. However, may I remind you that in 2004, Xavier Niel—who is now being courted by the whole of the political establishment—was for a short time held in custody for procuring, the same day as he was revolutionizing the market by launching the first Freebox at 19.99 euros a month—a fraction of the France Télécom rate at the time? And that the Logan is made in Romania, not in France. So I'm not so sure that the French welcoming committee for the frugal model would give it the warmest welcome in the world! Apart from the frugal approach,

2   A French Internet provider

the second element of major disruption is the maximization of Internet leverage, which is at the origin of 'uberisation.' The first to be affected have been commerce and tourism but all the other sectors will be impacted in one way or another. One of the surprises will doubtless come from the fact that these future developments will appear first of all in emerging countries, including China, before being imported into developed societies."

"I am thinking in particular of financial services. Twenty years ago, my banker friends were somewhat proud of the fact that, statistically, there was more chance of my getting divorced than of changing banks. Today, in the USA, of the Millennials—the generation born just before 2000—71% would rather go to the dentist than talk to a banker! According to a Capgemini study, 75% of Chinese who have bank accounts have already tried out the services of a fintech as compared to only 36% in France. If, during my mandate, I manage to get rid of the banking cartel— maybe following on the impetus of the Middle Kingdom—I'll be good for the Panthéon!"[3]

"One more figure to illustrate the point you are underlining, Mr. President: a five-year loan for the purchase of a consumer good costs a traditional commercial bank 7.5% of the sum lent in operational costs. On an on-line marketplace which puts a lender and a borrower in direct contact, this cost is only 2.5%. Therefore the platform can share with them the five points saved over the duration of the transaction. It is not only in Asia but in Africa that these new models are prone to mount the fastest assault on the inefficient cartels of traditional banks. In Kenya, for example, the government has launched the first bonds in the world to which the public can subscribe by cellphone only, thereby circumventing the banking sector. In Asia, the Western private banks who have set out to lay claim to the goldmine represented

---

3   Burial in the Panthéon in Paris is reserved only for those who have served France in some exceptional way.

by huge recently-acquired fortunes, have come up against some unexpected cultural difficulties. Only 10% to 20% of the wealthiest people use the services of private banks, the vast majority of them preferring to manage their financial future themselves, particularly through means provided by the Internet, and at a much lower cost. In a completely different field, the logistics sector should experience a revolution of the same magnitude as was the invention of the container ..."

"I recently met with the bosses of the Chronotruck company in France, which aims to reduce its delivery costs by 70% by means of better use of empty capacity—thanks to real-time awareness of demand changes in a specific geographical area. You see, in France too, we're brimming over with creative talent!"

"In China, the next breakthrough in the e-commerce revolution will be in that very sector—logistics—which accounts for 18% of GDP, double what it is in the West. It is all the more likely to be a source of productivity increases in that it will deal with new services linked to tracking. It is because it has the most highly-concentrated population in the world—particularly compared to the USA—that China should come out as the world leader in unit cost with regard to tracking services in the future."

"I talked about this with Frédéric Mazzella, the co-founder of BlaBlaCar, our national 'unicorn.' He explained that success of his idea by the absence of American competition. His car-sharing system can only work in areas of extremely dense population with excellent public transport and around central nerve points. These two elements are lacking in the USA, even in the large cities; the model works even less well in the USA because of the huge distances to be covered and low petrol costs."

"Mr. President, I am convinced that the more a service activity remains traditional in its thinking, the more it will be open to change in the near future. I think the best illustration of this is in the field of education which although, paradoxically, it is supposed to prepare our children for the future, is the one which remains the most deeply entrenched in outdated habits. We can make the same observation in the USA: in the course of the last three decades, costs in this sector have inflated even more spectacularly than in healthcare. The cost of schooling has increased three times faster than the rate of inflation as opposed to 'only twice' in the field of healthcare. The resulting paradox is that even students doing finance courses in the most prestigious universities do not realize that the return on investment in their studies is no longer attractive. This is shown by a default rate of 17% on the formidable mountain of 1.3 billion US dollars' worth of student loans—almost 10% of the American GDP. To my mind, the answer to this problem will undoubtedly come from China. It will boil down to one concept: online education, which China will have to take up at a much faster pace than other countries. Whereas I had classes in a room with 30 to 50 other students, the future will see classrooms of 500 to 1,000 students—tribute paid to a world whose population is doubling. Craig Wright, a leading light in classical music who taught at the prestigious Yale University in the USA, said, after one of his classes was put online just before he retired: 'I will have had more students in my last six months of teaching than during the whole of the rest of my career.' Actually, the future model will not be free classes from MOOCs—Massive Open Online Courses—but rather real training certificates spread over several months and leading to online diplomas promoted by recruiters. Results of initial experiments carried out by the most highly-renowned American institutions have been extremely promising."

"My dear chap, even in France, the dean of HEC[4] has told me how surprised he was to see a large number of brilliant young Af-

---

4   École des hautes études commerciales de Paris, the most prestigious french business school.

ricans enrolled in his online certificates, particularly from Ivory Coast, a country in the throes of rebirth. Apparently, the course content, which combines video lectures and weekly online discussions, gets feedback of a much higher quality because the teacher can focus any following lectures on points that students have not completely understood."

"China should be one of the main benefactors of online education. Officially, the country produces seven million graduates a year, but only 500,000 will have the privilege of going to study abroad—less than 10%. Even so, this is a formidable number to be assimilated by Western institutions when you consider that only 25,000 students are lucky enough to graduate from the universities of Oxford and Cambridge every year. Unfortunately for the vast majority of students remaining in the Chinese system, they have to put up with outdated teaching methods, even in the best universities. The answer is therefore to have online courses, which will be easy to set up particularly since a recent study by Crédit Suisse showed that, among the under-30s, 28% of young Chinese had already had some form of Internet schooling. I can see new avenues opening for our best schools if they can see their way to reinventing themselves. And online vocational training should be made available, including in English, particularly specializing in the new jobs created by the digital and environmental revolutions. What's more, this will mean that France will no longer be placed behind Australia in the Shanghai Ranking of the best universities in the world! But we shall have to be careful that the educational sector doesn't repeat the mistake made by the press, which has let Google almost monopolize the aggregation of its content, thereby leading to its demonetization. I can see it coming now—our best French schools putting their content at the disposal of the American agregator Coursera, which was unknown only a few years ago. I can't help worrying about the future economic model of our best training organizations and whether or not their management—who are supposed to be helping the younger generation to anticipate what's coming—have the necessary vision ... We may need to do a clean sweep of this so-called 'elite'—Chinese fashion!"

"And yet, I have heard that China put a halt to all its Executive MBA programmes in early 2016, particularly the ones that were in partnership with foreign universities—which was the only reason to wage an effective war against corruption in the system. The best solution, as we have said, is online diplomas that our best institutions can offer in total transparency with standards of excellence that would not bring the quality of our best schools and universities into question. I have already mentioned the initial online experiments which show that this new means of teaching would suit emerging countries perfectly."

"Provided that these schools don't get swallowed up on the web by Coursera which is preparing to inflict the same treatment on them as Google has for the press: skimming off 30% of the income without financing the content in any way."

"Well said."

The President turns to his communications adviser: "Anne, call France-Stratégie. I want a report on how to make our teaching establishments world leaders in online vocational training, starting with the French-speaking world. And, while you're doing it, summon the deans of our twenty leading institutions to the Élysée." He turns back to me with:

"Don't underestimate the changes that our system for training the *crème de la crème* will be going through: already last year, the *corps des ponts,*[5] which used to be highly prized, saw itself rele-

---

5   Corps of bridges: an elite body of civil engineers

gated to 271ˢᵗ place in the Polytechnique rating for recruitment, since the brightest elements preferred to start up their own businesses rather than take a suit-and-tie job in traditional industries. There's a revolution well under way among the younger generation and I intend to promote it during my mandate. We shall be paying tribute to four of the six founders of PayPal who each tried to blow up their high schools when they were 16!"

"I'm totally with you on that, Mr. President. But I must underline the issues facing education in China. Online teaching will make young Chinese people even more attracted to the economy of sharing. You only have to look at what makes up everyday meals in China—the dishes are in the middle of the table and are offered to all the guests. Chinese tourists coming to France always have trouble understanding how it is that we are content with only one individual dish when what the person sitting next to you is having also deserves to be sampled! In a recent survey, Nielsen found that 94% of Chinese were prone to sharing resources as opposed to only 43% of North-Americans. In order to understand the radical changes that this development may bring about, one needs look no further than the music industry: in the USA, streaming, with over a third of market share, is ahead of both downloads and physical purchases; but in China, in only two years, streaming alone accounts for 56% of the industry's revenue, proving once again that the speed at which the Chinese are adopting new digital behaviour patterns is twice that of the Americans!"

"Don't forget that China has gone directly—or almost directly—from the Stone Age to the golden age of capitalism, without passing through any intermediary stage. The Chinese are less locked into old habits than we are. This partly explains why they are embracing new technology with such fervor."

"That's precisely the advantage of the blank page approach. The opposite of what I call the 'Smart syndrome' which must be avoided at any cost: it's a concept that looks very attractive but is commercially disastrous. It was the ebullient Nicolas Hayek who was the first to realize that a city car in developed countries only carried 1.7 passengers on average. His engineers therefore had the idea of developing a small city car for only two people. After considerable initial success, he sold the company to the German group Daimler which undertook to increase production rates aggressively. A few years later, Daimler had to admit its failure publicly. Its investment was massively depreciated, causing losses of several billion euros. Their thinking had been all wrong because they had forgotten the original purpose of the car: to provide freedom of movement, not only for the driver but also for his or her family, particularly at weekends. Therefore the Smart car could only be a second car—a complement to the family car. And then, of course, it meant a second parking space at home and one at the workplace as well. In an urban context, this limited the potential market to certain bachelors or the privileged few. Commercial failure was a foregone conclusion."

"It's a well-known fact that, if you ask engineers to find a solution, their natural reaction is simply to try and modify what already exists. Just like my énarque advisers![6] Ask a blank page for a solution and it will think differently ..."

"For example, in terms of service and not of adding to the product. It was not the automobile product itself that was in question, but the way it was used. From this came the concept of car-sharing which one can sense is just beginning to gain ground in our societies. In France, almost 20% of the population is enrolled on the BlaBlaCar website, with the highest proportion naturally being the under-30s who see it as a natural means of getting from one place to another without having to own a vehicle."

---

6   Enarque is a graduate of ENA.

"I rather like your idea of the blank page, but you must admit that it is easier to implement in a country where the Cultural Revolution has wiped out the legacy of history. That's not the case in our country, and one mustn't forget that point, particularly since that is what Chinese tourists come looking for in France ..."

"Mr. President, nothing could be further from my thoughts than the idea of wiping out our past with a stroke of the pen and replacing it with a blank page. But is it really justified to abandon the building of a modern tower block in Paris, designed by our world-renowned star architect Jean Nouvel, on the grounds that the Eiffel Tower was erected over a century ago? In Hong Kong, the real estate developer Sun Hung Kai built a splendid 40-storey building in 1999, IFC One, and, because of its success, the same group built its big brother right next to it in 2003—the Two International Finance Center (IFC Two)—which was twice as high. And, while any sensible developer would have been happy to live on rental income for the rest of his life, just when the worst financial crisis since the 1930s was happening, the same group threw itself into the gargantuan International Commerce Centre (ICC) project, a building of 108 storeys soaring up into the airspace above. Opened in 2010, it is not located on Hong Kong island itself, but on the bay opposite in Kowloon—a historic district separated from the financial centre, Central. Nevertheless, this has not prevented ICC from now housing the offices of the bankers Morgan Stanley, Deutsche Bank and Crédit Suisse, whose bosses can celebrate their most profitable deals in the bar of the Ritz-Carlton Hotel on the top two floors of the tower. Three iconic buildings which reflect a triple gamble—each one more daring than the previous one—that the Sun Hung Kai group has managed to pull off."

The President turns to his advisers: "You will note, as I have, that the pioneering spirit of the USA in the 20th century has now come to roost in China in the 21ˢᵗ century, by way of Hong Kong ... which reminds me of that wonderful axiom of André Malraux: 'Culture is not inherited, it is conquered.'"

"Indeed, Mr. President, in China, heritage must always give place to conquest. Priority is always given to the future at the expense of the past. This is another, and by no means the least, of its paradoxes: a country governed by the old ... for the young!"

"Allow to me to point out that it is easier to build new buildings than to change mentalities. In politics, the pace of decision-making cannot be that of the world of property developers. Trump is going to find that out in the coming months ..."

"Maybe, Mr. President, but there is no real reason why, with your influence, we can't develop a new 'frugal' model. In Hong Kong, public expenditure is at 20% of GDP, roughly a third of the 57% spent in France. And yet, material and personal safety is totally guaranteed; the streets are cleaner than in Paris; the hospitals and the law courts work well; life expectancy is almost 85, the highest in the world, although only 5% of GDP is spend on healthcare; only high-level education is essentially in private hands. Three weeks after her election as head of the Île-de-France region, Valérie Pécresse was already able to announce a plan to make savings of 125 million euros, 5% of the region's budget, simply by getting rid of official cars and grants to so-called non-profit making associations whose operating costs were more than 40% of the amount of donations they received. This was not so much 'austerity' as marking the end of the mismanagement of the previous administration, which have not been prosecuted in any way—which would have been the case in China."

"Believe it when I say that I am more saddened than you are by the annual report of the National Audit Office; and what makes me even more indignant is the fact that, apart from some very rare exceptions, no remedial action is being taken with regard to this waste of public money. That's why I intend to hit hard during my mandate. I have not yet announced the measures, but, for example, I plan to take a look at the Global Fund To Fight Against AIDS: the French contribution has been renewed at over 1 billion euros over three years, ten times the Italian contribution which is more in line with the real achievements of this organization. That particular contribution is stretching the budget of the Foreign Ministry, which, in order to finance it, is having to sell off the cream of its real estate assets abroad ..."

"Like the recent sale of the French consul general's former residence in Hong Kong—a symbolic indicator for the Chinese leaders of the real state of our public finances."

"My dear chap, if you were in my shoes, you would realize that that's not really the problem. My concern comes rather from the fact that when the former President of the Unibail-Rodamco group, the indefatigable Guillaume Poitrinal—in his time the youngest-ever chief executive officer of the CAC40—was appointed by my predecessor to be in charge of the 'simplification shock,' he had to throw in the towel because of the difficulty in taking any action, even after asking publicly for 'a simplification of the simplification process'! Proof that an approach which takes the existing status as a starting point cannot fundamentally reform a system that employs twice as many civil servants as our German neighbors. This brings me to believe that the problem is not so much to ask an organization like the Economic and Social Council to bring its scandalous lifestyle down by a few percentage points, but rather it is to ask the question—falling in the line with Chinese 'frugal' reasoning you have been talking about—whether there is any real added value in the Council's reports, and, in case of a negative answer, to purely and simply abolish it. That is a case in point where I would replace it by your 'shadow cabinet' of a score or so of 25-year-olds who would try to combine the digital revolution with the public good!"

"It's true they might do a better job even of inventing a frugal model of direct democracy enabling you to identify the real concerns of your voters. That's what the Chinese government has done through the social media—Weibo in the past and WeChat today. Even though the Chinese Big Brother is of course inacceptable to us with our attachment to individual freedom, it at least has the advantage of enabling the government to identify what the largest population in the world sees as the main critical issues. In the end, it is the only way for it to ensure its legitimacy with more than a billion people—who didn't elect it. The digital revolution may well be being used to help the Chinese government to rethink the management of public services, but it is for private enterprise that it will prove to be most profitable."

The Great Leap Forward—Season 4.0

"When talking about China just now, you used the expression 'Great Leap Forward—Season 4.0.' I'm curious to know exactly what you mean by that."

"The largest infrastructure construction site in China today is the Three Gorges Dam, which took almost two decades to complete. Apart from the technical prowess it shows, the Chinese government is extremely proud of the fact that, when the first stage was carried out, the turbines all came from abroad, whereas, for the most recent stage, they were all made in China. This is proof that the technology transfer policy in force at the time was the most judicious. This is what strategy specialists call the 'copycat' approach. In the new upcoming phase of the digital revolution, China has decided to change horses. It no longer sees its future in merely copying the West, but intends to sinicize technological progress. Firstly, to cater better to its own needs, then to make an assault on the most inefficient sectors of the Western world, like the banking, pharmaceutical, agri-food, energy and defence industries."

"China's progress to date has been acknowledged in a recent study carried out under the auspices of the United Nations by the World Intellectual Property Organization (WIPO) in conjunction with INSEAD[7] and Cornell University. China has joined the top twenty five most innovating countries, and this is the first time that a developing country has achieved such a high ranking. Of the 50 companies with the highest values in the world, 31 still come from the USA, but 8 are now Chinese, heading up the 7 European ones."

"Following the same thread, China is already the big winner in one of the main industries of the future: mobile phone commerce, or m-commerce. It already accounts for 50% of China's e-commerce and should reach 71% by 2019, when the USA will only be at 22%, according to the market research company eMarketer. A quarter of the 'unicorns'—companies valued at over a billion dollars—involved in m-commerce are Chinese."

"Like you, I think that today the Internet is entering a new implementation phase in companies, particularly in the manufacturing sector. As a symbol of this, my friend Angela mentioned the recent alliance between Apple, leader of the smartphone field, and SAP, leader in software for enterprise resource planning. The company with the highest market capitalization in the world needs a German partner to order to take a major new direction, moving towards large industrial companies."

"It's in China that investment in technology has progressed most quickly in recent years—an exponential rise: 1 billion US dol-

---

7   The European Institute of Business Administration

lars in 2010, 11 billion in 2014, 36 billion in 2015 and a figure estimated at almost 50 billion for 2016. This is enough to revolutionize e-commerce, logistics and fintech ..."

"My attention has been drawn to the fact that Research and Development expenditure remained almost stable in Europe between 2007 and 2012, whilst it increased by almost 80% in China, reaching 2% of GDP, the equivalent of the European level, but with the objective of rising to 2.5% during the next five-year plan."

"The Shenzhen region just north of Hong Kong, which used to be called 'the workshop of the world,' is now repositioning itself as 'the laboratory of the world,' having already invested 4% of local resources in Research and Development. On a more general level, China accounts for 18% of world expenditure on Research and Development, particularly because multinationals have located 1,300 of their research centers there."

"A few years ago, some experts thought that China would be overtaken by India, because its political regime—a democracy—was more favorable to economic take-off than the Chinese 'dictatorship.' Obviously, this has not been the case. India only accounts for 2% of world R & D investment, which makes one fear that this is a country 'growing without development,' the perfect example of what General de Gaulle famously said about Brazil: 'A country that has a high potential and will keep having it for a very long time.'"

"Human capital is being enriched too. In 2020, China will have nearly 200 million graduates, the equivalent of the working population of the USA. Although they have not all been trained up to global levels, almost 500,000 a year are now benefiting from being educated abroad. And—an interesting fact—more than 80% return home after their studies whereas only a third did so in 2010. This goes against the erroneous idea, put about in the West, that there is a brain drain following the recent tightening-up on the political front."

"You said just now that preconceived ideas about capital outflow were also wrong. I would add that, even if 9,000 millionaires did in fact leave China in 2015, my predecessor achieved the feat of getting 10,000 to leave France in the same year. This information doesn't come from the Finance Ministry but from the research group New World Wealth."

"Getting back to Chinese students, Mr. President ... When they were asked by the Brookings Institution what motivated them to return to China, they answered: 'China is my home!.' This echoes what Simon Leys observed some years ago, with the slight nuance that, this time, motivation is not only spiritual, but material: the next revolution will be that of the Internet of Things, and China, because of its size, will be one of the critical defining world markets. We can already see this in electric cars: China is convinced it is in pole position and foresees producing 1.3 million vehicles in 2020—half of world production. The key challenge is to make running costs per kilometer ten times less than they are for a petrol vehicle. China will also make up for lost time compared to the USA with regard to the connected car."

"I have been struck by the fact that, in order to ensure connectivity and information flow, a car today contains one kilometer of fibre ... If 90% of vehicles are indeed to be connected by 2020, then China, which already produces almost double the volume produced in the USA, should be the main beneficiary."

"Let's look at what's happening in three key fields: the cloud, mobile phones and data analysis. The cloud has applied the principles of the sharing economy to the software sector, thereby cutting the cost of using servers and making them accessible even to small businesses. The explosion of income generated from this has mostly benefited the American giants, four of whom account for more than half of this highly coveted market. The leader, surprisingly enough, is Amazon, usually better-known for its e-commerce, which, however, is making more than half of its operational profits from the cloud. Its activities there are three times greater than those of its most direct competitor, Microsoft. But when it comes to the game of critical size, China knows very well that time is on its side. It has noted that the online payment system Alipay, a subsidiary of Alibaba, deals with a daily volume of transactions that is today ten times greater than that of the American PayPal. The same dynamic will determine the future of connected devices; even if, by 2020, they don't reach the sixty billion predicted by Cisco, they will be bound to invade our daily lives. The Chinese consumer electronics giant, Midea, has anticipated this very well by forging an alliance with Xiaomi—valued at almost 40 billion US dollars when it last raised funds—and with the German group Bosch, one of the jewels in the crown of European technology. By the way, it is interesting to note how a group like Xiaomi, portrayed in the Western press as just a manufacturer of cheap smartphones, considers itself to be a software company. Its research department employs six times more specialists in software than in hardware; it sees its future in the monetization of applications that use connected devices as a distribution network. And it already ranks second in the world behind the American Fitbit on the market for wearables—portable connected devices. In another field, the booming sector of air purifiers, the introduction of a sensor that tells you when to replace the filter, has enabled the Midea-Xiaomi alliance to improve the customer experience for its products and to gain almost a third of the Chinese market in under a year."

"Those examples are extremely impressive, I agree. I looked into the question of connected devices after talking recently with our compatriot, Luc Julia, who is based in California and heads up the Samsung Strategy and Innovation Centre, which is very active in this field. One thing in particular he told me was that none of these new objects taken separately was managing to maintain user interest for more than four months. He estimates that, in the end, these objects will only become established when they are connected within a network, communicating from machine to machine, as in the case of home automation. This is an opportunity for industrialist, who are looking to make the different components of production lines communicate with each other. Therefore the B2B market looks like taking off before the B2C market, so it is in this segment that our industrialists should position themselves. By the way, I am very glad to see that, in all sorts of places throughout the world, a large number of French scientists are playing a key role in the development of these technologies of the future."

"But very often they're working away from France, in Silicon Valley or elsewhere. For a young person keen on connected devices, remember that France today is 45th in the world ranking ..."

"Where do you get this ranking from?"

"It's France's ranking from early 2016 in *State of the Internet*, the quarterly report published by Akamai, the company that is the world specialist in Internet networks. The study is a reference work in the technology world and measures the effective average speed of Internet connections in each country."

"I read another report, the *EU Digital Agenda* produced by the European Union, which showed in 2015 a penetration rate for very high speed Internet access at 15% in France, exactly half the European average. Hardly surprising given our under-investment in telephone networks for ten years—18% less per inhabitant compared to the rest of the OECD, according to the OpenSignal company. For a long time, it was Italy's prerogative to be the country that lagged behind—already in the 1970s my parents were complaining about the state of Italian motorways ... Today, it is not motorways but the information highway that matters for the upcoming generation. Italy shows us the consequences of the explosive cocktail that awaits us if we don't react in time: a public debt exceeding 100% of GDP and zero growth for 15 years. The result: a very high speed internet penetration of only 5%. This is why, in my campaign, I have underlined the importance I attach to the telecommunications industry, and I fully intend to invest in its infrastructure—one of the flagships of my mandate."

"Mr. President, that is sure to please all our young French Internet users. But it won't stop them from thinking of you as the president of one of the few countries in the world that has increased taxation of the telecommunications industry in order to finance the huge losses made by public television—which, for a very long time already, the young have bequeathed to their grandparents. And they see, in France and in the rest of Europe, that any consolidation of the telecom sector is forbidden—a sector that still has 144 European operators, whilst China Mobile alone has 800 million subscribers, making it more likely to set the standards for the future norms of 5G technology, which will come next. And we cannot think only in terms of material infrastructure. The other force that will drive the future revolution will come from the explosion of data analysis. It will directly favor progress in artificial intelligence and open a vast field of hitherto unexplored possibilities, a field in which Google and Microsoft fully intend to indulge in fierce competition. Mathematics are going to enrich our daily lives as never before ..."

"Don't worry. That message has already been delivered to me, in brilliant fashion, by that clever man Cédric Villani, our Fields medal winner, who gave me his book, *Théorème du Vivant*.[8] He explained to me how mathematics are now winning over new fields of application. He told me: 'The digital revolution has not yet transformed our daily lives, it's just beginning. The surprises will not come from our computers' speed of calculation, but from the qualitative improvement in the treatment of huge amounts of low-quality data.' So, in industrial sectors, new algorithms will enable us to test up to five million different exploitation patterns in the space of only 24 hours, and this will revolutionize, for example, the oil exploration sector."

"Contrary to what many people think, it is not the Americans but the Chinese who make the most money out of data. The social media WeChat, which belongs to the Tencent group, gets seven times more revenue per subscriber than its American competitor WhatsApp—even though it belongs to Facebook who acquired it for the modest sum of 20 billion US dollars. Today, WeChat has almost 700 million subscribers for whom it is becoming more and more a sort of private concierge. Because of its platform of unique applications, it caters to almost all ordinary everyday needs. WeChat is the most developed of the 'strong links,' a platform which enables you to create groups of friends and family as you need them. These are well targeted communities which make a high value-added content exchange possible— quite the opposite of Facebook's generalist approach. WeChat is bringing yesterday's business models up to date, transforming each Chinese person into someone who sells products to his friends, with commission, just like the 1960s American housewife did with Tupperware ..."

"On the industrial front, it seems obvious to me that none of our multinationals can ignore the potential of Big Data any more: the heads of Sanofi told me why they joined up with Google in

8   Theorem Of The Living World

order to analyze relevant data on people with diabetes. This disease now accounts for the largest area of medical expenses—12% of global healthcare costs."

"What's more, the disease is progressing in China more than anywhere else, with 110 million sufferers. As for obesity, this already affects 25% of the population—a result of high-speed urbanization and the disastrous food habits of the one-child generation. For the most innovative brains, this data revolution is going to open new fields of invention linked to connected devices, connectivity networks, software platforms and app development. The chosen few will be very few, because the 'winner takes all' rule will still continue to operate, as it does today when, on Apple Store, 1% of applications generate 94% of revenue. China won't be left behind, because it intends to use the scale effect of its population to the full."

"Let's go on to the objectives of this trip to China. I may have upset protocol and slightly annoyed the German Chancellor by not rushing to Berlin as soon as I was elected, but I wanted to send a signal to that lady. China cannot remain the preserve of the Germans. I know that our dear Angela goes there at least once a year. Our embassy in Beijing keeps me informed of the innumerable economic events organized by the Germans throughout China and in which they show off their technology as well as their agricultural products. Even if a little cold water has been poured on their ardors recently, for reasons we mentioned earlier, it seems to me that very strong common interests are being sketched out between Germany and China in the fields of industrial automation and robotics—in other words, what our German friends call industry 4.0. All that is part of the great Chinese plan for industrial modernization: *Made in China 2025*. I wouldn't like to see France remain on the touchline ..."

"Clearly, Mr. President, *Made in China by China for China* is the government's central objective. This is the benchmark by which we have to evaluate the acquisition of the German robotics leader Kuka by the Chinese giant Midea for almost 4.5 billion euros in cash in the spring of 2016—something we have already talked about. Robotisation is one of China's priorities in order to respond to the productivity challenge. Half the world's growth in industrial automation and robotics over the next five years will take place in China. It's true that, in Chinese factories at the moment, there are only 36 robots for every 10,000 workers, as opposed to 192 in Germany, 314 in Japan and 478 in South Korea. But, at the present time, 35% of all patents linked to robotisation are being taken out in China. The Taiwanese company Foxconn, Apple's main supplier, intends to replace up to 30% of its workforce by robots within five years. The 3D printing sector should grow from 4 billion US dollars at present to 20 billion in 2020, redefining production processes in industries such as automobiles, aeronautics, defense and medical technology. The American company General Electric foresees that, by 2020, half of its spare parts will be 3D printed. These are all strategic sectors in which China wants to play a leading role, as in the semiconductor industry, a crucial link in these new value chains. The problem for the Chinese is that they consume about 100 billion US dollars' worth of semiconductors every year, which they put into their computers and smartphones and which are then re-exported. But they only produce about 6% to 7% of these semiconductors. Importing them costs more than importing oil. The government particularly wants China to position itself on the semiconductor market of the future. But this strategy is coming up against strong opposition from the USA and from Europeans. As you have pointed out, several attempts to acquire semiconductor manufacturers over the past few months have been blocked: Fairchild, Micron, Lattice Semiconductor in the USA and Aixtron in Germany. These companies work partly for the

Pentagon and it is out of the question for the US administration to let such sensitive technology go to China. An underground war is being waged, in which China has obviously not said its last word. It envisages increasing its global market share in semiconductor production from 10% today to 45% by 2025. Tsinghua Unigroup, which is associated with the prestigious Tsinghua University in Beijing, apparently has an investment plan involving 80 to 100 billion US dollars to ensure the future Chinese domination of the new generation. Tsinghua Unigroup is an astonishing company, by the way: in 2009 its assets totalled only 30 million US dollars, but reached 6 billion towards the end of 2015 ..."

"I can sense this robotics fever coming to our shores. For the moment, the general public only sees the fun side of it: when I went on a recent visit to the SNCF,[9] I was welcomed not by the CEO but by Pepper, a little robot that one might suppose to have feelings because it asked me how I was and if I was in a good mood ... I should remind you that Pepper is the fruit of French creative genius—from the Aldebaran company which, a few years ago, fell into the hands of the Japanese Softbank company, which has just allied itself with the Taiwanese specialist in mass production, Foxconn, and the Chinese e-commerce giant, Alibaba. I'm sure we haven't seen the last of Pepper with regard to our daily lives! But I'm no fool: the aim behind the robotisation of factories is—in the short or long term—to get rid of the human element on production lines and even in offices by means of artificial intelligence. Now, as President of the Republic, I have to concern myself with the social consequences of this progressive automation of labor, which doesn't only affect blue-collar workers but executives and licensed professionals as well. What can I say to our people? That it's a trend that can't be stopped? That

---

9   SNCF (Société nationale des chemins de fer français) is the The French national railway company

jobs will disappear? That, thanks to vocational training a car factory operative will be transformed into a creator of algorithms? That it will come down to the concept of a guaranteed income for all, which was such a hot topic during the presidential election campaign?"

"Mr. President, I have no doubt that you are going to have to deal with quite an outcry. It may not go so far as throwing robots into the Seine—the way weavers threw machines into the river under Louis-Philippe—but the issue of replacing manpower by machines will be yet more fodder for the 'experts.' I have no doubt that your advisers have already told you that, during the last decade, only 10% of job losses in the USA were caused by outsourcing to China, as against 90% by automation. And, in spite of all this, the USA have managed to get back to a level of job creation that has reached 200,000 a month. Delaying the automation revolution will only aggravate our industry's loss of competitiveness. To my mind, the solution is to conceive of new services that will arise from these changes and significantly increase training programmes for employees who fall victim to technological development. But you shouldn't listen to me on this subject, but rather to Stefan Löfven, the Swedish Prime Minister, who has said publicly in Davos that the best thing that ever happened to him was losing his job as a young metalworker when his factory closed down."

"I hear what you say, but all that can't be done just by clicking your fingers. What concerns me—and I think it's the same for all my counterparts in developed countries—is how the middle classes will fare. How can we escape the 'elephant chart' produced by the economist Branko Milanovic? It shows how income has grown over recent years in relation to global wealth. The curve looks like an elephant's profile: it goes up from left to right then comes down and goes up again like the pachyderm's trunk. Interpretation: there is an initial acceleration in the increase in global income for the poorest 50%—the main beneficiaries of the insertion of emerging countries into the world economy thanks to globalization; the same goes for the richest 10%—capitalists who profit from the new arbitrage between automation and labor costs; however, for the 50% to 90% in the middle—in fact the middle classes of developed countries—they see the slowest increase in income because of industrial outsourcing to countries where costs are lower. Hence the concomitant rise of populism on both sides of the Atlantic. Whilst there has been hope that these developments would be damped down thanks to relocations or reindustrialization, you tell me that automation will be attacking the middle class even before it can fully develop in emerging countries like China. With a new boomerang effect on developed economies."

The President turns to his economic adviser: "Édouard, we have to urgently speed up our work on setting up the huge plan for online training aimed at professional reorientation towards the new jobs in the digital field. Unemployment benefit must be linked to online certification that qualifies people in the skills required for all these new jobs. We don't want another Alstom happening! If we succeed, we'll cut unemployment in half, as they've done in Germany—which is still in first place with regard to vocational training. If we fail, it is quite likely that I'll be handing over the house keys to Marine[10] in five years time.

"I don't know if this will help to console you, Mr. President, but remember that the fate of the middle classes is an issue in almost all the countries in the world. You'll see that it will become a central theme for the work of the G20 ..."

The President calls over his economic adviser once again: "Édouard, in the notes about China, forget once and for all the usual stuff on

10   Marine Le Pen, leader of the National Front Party

excess capacity of the steel industry, the amount of coal used in energy production and agricultural reform, etc. Concentrate on the technological revolution and its social consequences. I want regular reports on how the Chinese are going to avoid the implosion of society in a country in which 21ˢᵗ century robots will coexist with a population half of whom are still living in a rural world and in conditions that are more like those of the 19ᵗʰ century."

Careful! There's more to China than meets the eye!

"Mr. President, I see that the London *Financial Times* has pride of place on top of your pile of newspapers on the table. You will doubtless remember that the paper was purchased a few years ago by the Japanese media group Nikkei, for the staggering sum of 1.3 billion US dollars. By the way, that makes 2.5 million US dollars per journalist, which shows that competent journalists are still worth more than any old blogger. Up until the eleventh hour, it was the German company Axel Springer—the only European media group to have managed to switch to the digital world—that was due to acquire it. They were planning to build a real European digital platform of financial information capable of rivaling its American competitors. However, the owners—the English group Pearson—preferred at the last minute to sell to the Japanese at a considerable premium, even though the latter had no experience in digitalization and had never ventured outside Japan."

"We know the English well enough to know they will always sell their body and soul to the highest bidder!"

"Naturally! But why would the Japanese pay such an amount for a British newspaper when their compatriots have the greatest of problems expressing themselves in the language of Shakespeare? Simply because they saw the FT as the most anti-Chinese newspaper with a worldwide reputation. Only 1.3 billion dollars to keep up the daily discouragement of a large number of decision-makers in the world from taking any interest in China—that seemed like a bargain to the Japanese!"

"One US dollar per Chinese citizen and you get what you want in counter-propaganda ... Put like that, a very reasonable price indeed!"

"So your advisers are being served up a daily menu from the FT consisting of a 'problem platter' with Japanese sauce, portraying a China that is cash-strapped, corrupt, aging, polluted, indebted ... It certainly reflects part of the truth. But if I may make a suggestion, do what I do: for each *Financial Times* you read, read a *China Daily* as well—the Chinese government's propaganda organ. You will conclude that there may be more to China than meets the eye. It may well continue to create more than ten million new jobs a year, but it's also going to destroy more than ten million at the same time and, in so doing, pay splendid homage to the economist Joseph Schumpeter and his theory of creative destruction. Last week I called a Chinese friend of mine whom I've known for a long time to ask for his opinion of the present situation. He summed up his country's future in this equation: 'E > D + D?.' This means: 'Will the Entrepreneurship manage to overcome Debts and Demography?' or, will the proverbially dynamic Chinese character manage to absorb the huge accumulation of debt and trump the negative effects of demographic developments? According to my Chinese friend, China's greatest strength—hugely underestimated by the West—is women. It is Chinese women who manage families and who are the most entrepreneurial in the world. According to the Cyberspace Administration of China, 55% of Internet start-ups in China are founded by women. In the USA, only 22% of new companies have a woman as one of their founders. Go and ask Travis Kalanick, the founder of Uber: in China, he lost out to Jean Lui, the woman President of Didi Chuxing, his Chinese competitor! Jean Lui is the exceptionally talented daughter of the founder of the Lenovo group, Liu Chuanzhi, who brought her up on the principle of 'Expect things to be tough.'"

The President turns again to his economics adviser: "Édouard, check with the Ministry of Social Affairs to make sure that we have adequate measures to assist women in founding companies. Perhaps we could come up with something more imaginative or more radical? The women I know seem highly effective in catching on to changes in society and inventing new services to respond to them. There is a mine of new jobs to be found here."

"I have to say, Mr. President, that I really appreciate that equation. And it is just as relevant to our own country. Since we cannot really have any effect on demography in the short term, only a spectacular upturn in entrepreneurship will enable us to climb over the wall of debt and avoid defaulting on it. If this doesn't happen, this would be a lamentable admission of failure. This would then be the only option left to get wealth transferred from the old to the young—indebtedness residing essentially in the hands of pension funds—so that the upcoming generation could then rebuild the country."

"In China, entrepreneurship is the key—an improbable paradox that one has to accept. The country is capable of constructing—on credit—the greatest industrial excess capacity in the world: one billion one hundred tonnes of steel, twice the domestic demand; almost three billion tonnes of cement, 30 times more than the annual production of the USA ... And, at the same time, China is seeing world leaders emerge in the industries of the future, like Huawei in telecommunications. Huawei is now investing over 5 billion US dollars a year in research and development—15% of its turnover and more than its biggest European competitor, Ericsson in Sweden. Huawei is even aiming at a fivefold increase in its consumer division turnover—rising to 100 billion US dollars in five years' time—making it the world number one. You can find the same ambition at DJI, the world leader in drones. It is based in Shenzhen, which is also where BGI, the Beijing Genomics Institute, is building the world's largest genome sequencing capacity. Another thing to bear in mind is that Chinese business leaders often come up with rather iconoclastic managerial ideas. The *Harvard Business Review*, which can hardly be accused of communist sympathies, has just made a study of the management style of Haier, the Chinese consumer electronics group. Its president—following the 'frugal' line of thought—decided to turn each link in the value chain into a subsidiary, each subsidiary thus becoming autonomous and free to go after markets outside the group, which itself is allowed to have recourse to other suppliers if they are thought to be more competitive. This is a very innovatory approach and puts the whole organization under permanent pressure."

"I admire your enthusiasm for the New China, my friend ... By the time we land, you will have ended up convincing me that it's almost a model for France to follow ... Can you imagine the look on the faces of my ministers if I decided to launch such a Cultural Revolution in France? But embracing modernity as China is doing cannot hide the fact that the country still has a large number of weaknesses, isn't that right?"

"Is there a soft(ware) option?"

"Mr. President, if you manage to find a free hour during your time in Beijing, get yourself a foot massage at your hotel. You'll see how your feet affect the whole of the body. But let me warn you: choose the '*soft! soft!*' version of the massage, or else it'll be torture. It's the same problem in the New China. Its future rests on its ability to evolve towards soft-ware in order to strengthen its position—which, in hardware, is often as strong as the USA's position, including in the military field. Today, China only spends 20 billion US dollars each year on developing software—only 5% of such investment worldwide. Whereas American venture funds devote 20% of their investments to SAAS—Software As A Service—that is to say, software available on demand, which comes out much cheaper because costs are shared between a great many users, their Chinese counterparts only devote 2% of their investments to this, ten times less. This is a highly significant weakness in a domain that will be essential in the near future."

"But isn't this mainly because there has never been any copyright protection?"

"You're quite right to say that such protection is necessary for software development. In China, this is a field where the impressionistic touch still prevails, rather than a precise legal framework. But there are some positive signs emerging. In 2014, out of almost a thousand Intellectual Property law suits, 90% were won by the plaintiffs and 75% of court decisions were actually carried out. For one simple reason: Chinese companies are taking out more and more patents. They are therefore the main beneficiaries of this new policy. However, the legal successes of foreign countries in China are generally rapidly cut short, for the anti-monopoly commission can impose extremely heavy fines along the way. In the case of the American company, Qualcomm, 975 million US dollars in fines!"

"I am still convinced that the outcome of the software war will be in the West's favor. Over 90% of so-called triadic patents—i.e. valid in the USA, Europe and Japan—come precisely from these three geographical areas: 35% from the USA, 31% from Europe and 25% from Japan. A very large number of them include a software element. The outsourcing of software creation is therefore not advancing at the same pace as industrial operations."

"But, Mr. President, that doesn't mean that this situation is going to last. Western groups must remain vigilant and be careful of the 'IBM syndrome.' For twenty years, IBM preferred to keep its share price at an artificially high level through the use of buy-backs whose value was twice that of its Research and Development budget. Its turnover today is at the same level as it was in 1998. And the group has missed out on the major changes in the sector, such as the cloud, mobile phones, security and data analysis. So China is not necessarily helpless in face of the American giants."

"I'm well aware of that! In France, the extremely small and ultra-exclusive club of Doctors of Mathematics gets richer every year, and some of them are real geniuses. Yet last year I heard that the research centre of one of the largest Chinese groups managed to hire almost all of those who had decided to go into the private sector ..."

"In one way, Mr. President, we should be delighted! It proves that China still needs the West."

"IN THE WEST WE TRUST"

"How time flies in your company! What shall we drink with our dessert? I would suggest a glass of Château La Tour Blanche. First of all because it's an excellent and undeservedly little-known *premier cru* sauternes; secondly because it was gifted to the French government a century ago as part of the Osiris Donation.[1] This should remind the world that, even though France may have too many debts, it still has some very fine assets. We don't stand naked like the English after all their privatizations! But let's get back to China. I've been alerted to the rise of anti-Western feeling in the speeches of certain leaders, warnings of a return to imperialism, and I wonder what is behind it, since China will be needing foreign technology in the years to come ... Isn't it paradoxical to see the Chinese pushing the West out of China at the very moment when, if I understand you correctly, they are going to have the greatest need of it in order to improve their productivity?"

"Mr. President, that is art of negotiation—Chinese fashion. Actually, increased standards of living will naturally bring the people to invent a new way of life for themselves, partly inspired by the best of the West, and particularly by Europe. The economy will only prosper if a real service culture develops there, and this doesn't come naturally to the Chinese. Imported technology will only work with know-how that the Chinese will be obliged to come and get from us. For the Westerner—particularly for the French person—who seizes on these opportunities, China has never been such an exciting place! But to keep one's faith in the West, one has to look at the world in a dynamic not a static way."

---

1   A 1907 bequest in the will of the philanthropist Daniel Iffla, known as Osiris

A new wave of life

"Do you really think the lifestyle of the Chinese will become so westernized? Where's that frugality you are always talking about?"

"You've brought up a crucial point here: China is not going to get westernized. But one has to think in terms of 'way of life' rather than 'lifestyle.' A way of life starts in childhood with schooling, goes on to adult life with culture in the widest sense of the word, and ends with old age and any new trends arising from it. As far as schooling is concerned, we have already talked about the way digitalization is changing it. It will affect all levels, including vocational training and retraining which is essential for China. Curiously enough, I am not thinking so much about ENA—which I believe, because of its double costs in Paris and Strasbourg, is virtually bankrupt—but more about Xavier Niel's École 42 which has exported its model as far as California, in spite of California's supposedly being the pinnacle of technological know-how. Perhaps, during your stay, you could try and get some free real estate in Shanghai for Niel. This would do more for our country's influence than just talking about *French Tech*.

"Excellent idea!"

The President turns to his industrial adviser: "François, call Niel as soon as we arrive. In Shanghai I have a 30-minute interview scheduled with the mayor. Arrange for Niel to be on Skype at the same time and maybe he'll manage to do the California trick again. If all goes well, we won't just get some free land out of it but maybe the building as well! That will be more productive than giving the mayor an earful of French Tech—after all, we're the only ones in the world who ever talk about it. A lot of start-up founders tell me that we are still the laughing stock of the planet; it just proves that we can't think of technology today as being intrinsically borderless."

"Let me go on with my line of thinking about the 'way of life,' Mr. President. This is an immense opportunity for our tourism and leisure industry. Over twelve million Chinese tourists come to Europe every year, each spending between 2,500 and 3,000 euros on shopping. It's only been a short while since they've been able to benefit from the Alipay mobile phone payment system—produced in collaboration with the leading French company Ingenico. These figures will keep increasing rapidly in the future. Today, Europe only attracts 10% of Chinese travelers. In France, in the near future, we shall go from one to five million Chinese visitors every year, and yet Paris only has 16 million hotel nights in annual capacity. In fact, it's a Chinese entrepreneur, Wu Qin, the 'hotelier with four arms,' who seems to have best anticipated this demand. With his 800 rooms in the east of Paris, he always has a room number 520 on each floor of his hotels. The pronunciation of '520' in Chinese is the same as 'I love you,' which attracts the highly-coveted honeymoon trade in the most romantic capital in the world."

"Paradoxically, it seems once again that it's the Chinese who have taken best advantage of our potential!"

"Yes, indeed, Mr. President. The wealthiest man in China, Wang Jianlin, President of the property developer Dalian Wanda which has now switched to the entertainment industry, has linked up with Immochan, the real estate subsidiary of the Auchan group, to build a huge theme park in the 2020s near Roissy aimed mainly at catering to a Chinese clientele. This is a way of attacking the Euro Disney monopoly, taking its inspiration from the Hong Kong precedent where the Chinese-style theme park Ocean Park has always stopped the local Disneyland from getting off the ground. As for the aging population, it will give rise to new needs which the country is not suitably prepared for. We've already mentioned care of the elderly. But prevention of illness also offers numerous possibilities. No one has understood this better than our compatriot Decathlon, which has well anticipated the rise of sport as a source of well-being. The number of people taking part in marathons doubled in China between 2011 and 2014, reaching one million five hundred thousand runners. Xi Jinping has decreed that, henceforward, football will have national priority, just a few weeks after television rights for future World Cups were acquired by the same Wang Jianlin, and while the Madrid and Milan football clubs now fly the Chinese flag."

"I think the cases of the Olympique Lyonnais and AJ Auxerre are just a beginning. The Chinese government sees all this as part of its hope to improve footballing performances in the country and as a means of encouraging the Chinese to pay more attention to physical fitness. And I see that Xi Jinping is also thinking about organizing one of the future World Cups. We should be pleased about this, if this enables our clubs to have the financial means to become competitive again on a European level."

"In the same way, Mr. President, if our meal is anything to go by, food is an integral part of our way of life. In this respect, the Chinese still have a long way to go, even if this is beginning to change. Since the scandal of the melanin in baby milk in 2008, Chinese people have made food safety one of their hobbyhorses on the social media. Europe has an enormous advantage over the USA in terms of credibility on this issue. It is surprising that no serious academic research on the food industry has been carried out in the USA during recent decades. Harvard University offers no major in foodtech research. Certainly, American investment in agricultural technology has doubled recently, between 2014 and 2015, reaching 4.6 billion US dollars, but this remains a very modest sum compared to the country's expenditure on research, all the more since 30% of greenhouse gas emissions are linked to the food industry."

"I notice that the most talented financier in the world, Warren Buffett, continues to invest in 'junk food'—from Coca-Cola to Heinz. He is backing continual cost reductions rather than new consumer trends. It is Europe and not the USA that will come up with the sustainable nutrition of the future. Junk food explains the fact that the average height of the American population has stopped increasing since the 1970s, whilst it continues to increase in the rest of the world. Furthermore, I shall tell Xi Jinping that his grandchildren may very well turn out be grow taller than Trump's! An argument that Chinese pride cannot fail to be moved by. In a country such as ours, expenditure on food accounted for 30% of household budgets in 1960. It fell to only 12% in 2008, mostly to the benefit of expenditure on housing, which rose from 10% to 30% during the same period. Personally, I think that business activities linked to food constitute an enormous opportunity for our country. But this also means that our agri-food industry will have to be reformed. I was struck by a recent TNS Sofres survey during the Paris International Food Fair, which showed that, out of 14 countries polled, including France, two-thirds of consumers on average believed that it was 'probable that food was harmful to their health.' Food brands are going to have to do a lot of work to win them back, and not only in China!"

"Especially if they want our food products to be bought online, as 40% of Chinese already do, compared to only 10% of Americans."

"I conclude from your words that from cradle to grave, the European way of life is on its way to winning over the rest of the world. To my mind, both the USA and the Chinese are still unstable 'teens' who regularly have to look to their parents—Europe—to find a meaning in life. After all, Mao said that the USA of his time was: 'To be despised for its strategy; to be respected for its tactical sense.'"

"Mr. President, remember when Pope Francis went to the USA in September 2015. The same week, Xi Jinping also visited Uncle Sam. A sort of contest of the giants in the 'super-heavyweight' category, because each one represented a community of one billion three hundred million devotees. The result of the match: a technical knockout! The Pope's speech to Congress specifically called the country to order in moral matters and will go down in American history as one of the memorable moments of the Obama presidency; whilst Xi Jinping's speech went largely unnoticed."

"I am convinced that Europe certainly has its word to say in correcting the 'malfunction of the world,' to coin the phrase used by our academician Amin Maalouf. Your remarks about the Pope remind me of something I read recently about the Vatican remaining the leading nation in the world as far as wine consumption per person goes."

Turning to his communications adviser, the President says: "Anne, don't forget to remind me to mention the positive effects of wine on virtue at the next Paris Agricultural Show. Just like this delicious Château La Tour Blanche, which is a definite aid to spiritual thinking!"

"Mr. President, quote the Pope in France by all means, but it would be better not to quote him to your Chinese contacts. On the other hand, insist on the benefits of the European way of life and on our service culture, which is just asking to be exported."

"Don't worry, I shall avoid putting my foot in it, as Ségolène[2] did, dressed all in white on the Great Wall, when in China white is the color of mourning and death! The Chinese government has already let me know that they are very appreciative of my visit, coming as it does before I even visit Berlin. In fact, they are

---

2 Ségolène Royal, a socialist politician and presidential candidate in 2007.

delighted: imagine, the first official French visit for fifteen years without Raffarin![3]

"Is service included?"

"Mr. President, you almost certainly won't have the occasion to realize this during your short stay, but tips don't exist in China, in complete contrast to the USA where tipping has become a thinly disguised compulsory surtax. Traditionally, the Chinese don't pay for anything intangible, including restaurant service. This hardly encourages people to put their heart into their work. One could well understand this attitude in a country where it was considered noble to produce coal or steel but in a country that sees itself as the world's laboratory, habits are going to have to change. Contrary to industrial activities, services don't lend themselves very well to centralized planning."

"That's exactly why the country must be a testing ground for French service companies. They are a driving force of our economy with companies that truly lead the world. Provided that they understand China and manage to get their services paid for ..."

"Mr. President, I believe that the Chinese will be won over in time, for they realize the added value of these services. Let me illustrate my point by taking the example of culture. At the moment in China, there is a new museum opening every day. Some show great architectural prowess, and in some cases are the work of French architects, like the Lhassa Natural Science Museum in Tibet or the City History Museum in Beijing. The only problem is that most of these splendid building have no works to exhibit because of, among other things, the ravages of the Cultural Revolution. The Chendu MOCA—the Museum of Contemporary Art—has already fallen into disrepair because of corruption

---

3   Jean-Pierre Raffarin, a former conservative Prime Minister.

problems, only a few years after its much-heralded inauguration in 2011. At the same time, the Centre Beaubourg-Georges Pompidou in Paris can only show about 1% of its permanent collection of 120,000 artworks in a year."

"Please don't bring that up! Unfortunately, it's a widespread problem: the Quai Branly Museum of Primitive Arts has 'only' 50,000 artworks in stock and, like Beaubourg, exhibits only 1% of them every year. Quai Branly is mainly financed out of public funds and its annual grant is going to cost me the trivial sum of 42 million euros!"

"Exactly, Mr. President—what a potential to be exploited! Why not lend more and more to Chinese museums? In London, the Tate Modern is the only museum on the planet to figure among the top ten most-visited in the world while not a historic institution. And this despite the fact that, when it was opened, its permanent collection comprised only a few thousand works of art, including many that were of only minor interest. It has built its success on temporary loans from private collections never seen before, notably thanks to a strategic partnership with the Union Bank of Switzerland. An innovative idea that came from a management that is fully aware of the swing from modern art to contemporary art—which opened the field of exhibitions to new forms such as installations, and to new horizons, particularly towards emerging countries. Thus the great entry hall of this former power station has celebrated the works of innovative artists as diverse as the Chinese Ai WeiWei, the Dane Olafur Eliasson with the artificial sun of his *Weather Project*, the German Carsten Höller with his *Test Site* installations, the American Louise Bourgeois with her giant spider, and the Indian Anish Kapoor. The result: almost five million visitors a year, as opposed to three million five hundred thousand for Beaubourg which has been relegated to bottom of the list for multi-country exhibitions. All this with a budget for the Tate Modern that is 70% financed by private funds ..."

"Like you, I think it's less a question of means than of entrepreneurial qualities. The example of the Louvre in Abu Dhabi should stop being thought of as an exception. By the way, I expressed my deep gratitude to the emir for his decision to postpone the inauguration for several months after work had been completed on it, so as not to come into contact with my predecessor. The success of this project must be imitated by large numbers of our museums, by establishing partnerships in China. There remains the fear that, if we lend them our national treasures, they might send us back splendid copies in place of the originals ... But, you will say, that problem is not a new one. Wilhelm von Bode, the art historian specializing in Rembrandt, has been pleased to remind us that 'out of the seven hundred pictures painted by Rembrandt, about three thousand are still in circulation today.'"

"The interest of the wealthy Chinese for art is growing massively, whether it be antiques, modern art or contemporary art. This can be extremely annoying at times, I must confess. Maybe you had the time to read an astonishing interview with Wang Wei about a year ago in the *Financial Times*. She is the leading buyer of art in the world, famous for making a record bid in any public auction in order to acquire Modigliani's *Nu couché* [*Reclining Nude*] in 2015 for the modest sum of 170 million US dollars. It is an exceptional masterpiece and is destined for the Long Museum that she and her husband Liu Yiqian have opened in Shanghai. When asked about her criteria for choosing works, she replied: 'I only buy what is on the covers of Christie's and Sotheby's catalogues. After all, they can't put a fake on the cover!' Her husband, a former taxi driver who has made millions out of finance, interrupted the interview to add: 'Send this message to the West: we have bought your buildings and your companies, now we're buying your art!' Since she concedes at the end of the interview that she finally fell in love with her husband after their third child, one could say that, even in China, art can help soothe the mind!"

"I remember what the Queen of England said to the woman police officer in charge of the Chinese delegation's security during Xi Jinping's state visit to London: 'Bad luck! They were very rude!'"

"Quite honestly, one mustn't make generalizations. In communist China, people were fighting to survive. Everything was a struggle and there was scarcely any place for politeness or fine sentiments. As the middle class evolves into a group wishing to carve out a more harmonious life for itself, there will be more room for personal development. All human societies have experienced this. That's why everything to do with education constitutes a real opportunity for us.

It is all part of the new trend in consumption which is moving from the product to the service, from the service to the experience and from the experience to transformation. In the luxury sector, customer experience now accounts for over half of expenditure. These important—personalized—moments aim to change people's lives, whether it be by means of themed cultural experiences, retreats or meditation. So let's not limit the scope of our actions to vocational training alone, even if that constitutes the greatest opportunity. Every head of a major brand in China, particularly in Hong Kong, dreams of recruiting and keeping a local sales force that is truly competitive. It's a daily headache. China has built almost 4,000 shopping centers, but only a quarter are professionally managed according to Dalian Wanda, the country's leading property developer. To counter the offensive of e-commerce, these high-end centers are trying to develop a new 'e(motional)-commerce.' They have created specific emotions thanks to the new technologies of image processing and virtual reality ... We have the technology, the experience, the know-how and the teaching establishments. There is a real highway opening before us ... So let's get on to it!"

"I completely agree with you. Even if the Chinese leaders keep saying that they are the most competent in the world, it's easy to see that they lack know-how. The Tianjin disaster in the summer of 2015 is a particularly striking example: sets of rules exist, and they are even very stringent, occasionally even more so than in our own countries. The only problem is that they are never observed. So, in the water sector, no less than fifteen different organizations share governance, which waters down all responsibility. What the country needs, in a case like Tianjin, is not so much technology but know-how with regard to project management and resource coordination. Even if China has a natural reluctance to open up its market to us, it will end up coming to terms with this if we prove that it's in its interest to do so."

"That's precisely the reason why the American social media LinkedIn is so successful in China. Officially, social media are closed to foreigners. However, since the disappearance of the French media Viadeo, LinkedIn has established itself there—the only foreign social media to do so—thanks to a joint venture with China Capital. After less than two years' presence, it now has almost 20 million members, drawn from the up-and-coming elite of the country—a market that LinkedIn's bosses estimate at 150 million white-collar workers. This success comes from the fact that LinkedIn's management have demonstrated to Chinese leaders the advantages of finding the best possible match between supply and demand for qualified jobs for the seven million graduates who come out of the education system every year. If they don't find the jobs they are seeking, their growing frustration would create the potential risk of social unrest in the long term. This has to be taken particularly seriously in a country where the Academy of Social Sciences has counted 180,000 demonstrations in one year. This is not sufficiently underlined in the West: China is not a dictatorship with a population that just follows orders!"

"Let's be realistic here: the challenge for Western companies is immense. Specifically because the Chinese leaders never cease to be delighted about having closed off their country to the American Internet giants and thereby enabling Chinese companies to lead the field. This is the opposite of European policy, which has witnessed Europe's submission to American supremacy. Today, the three Chinese giants in the sector—Tencent for social media, Alibaba for e-commerce and Baidu the search engine—are the only companies in the world of a similar size to their American competitors. This policy is the extreme opposite of the one that is in force with regard to China's industrialization which has resorted to foreign investment in a big way. In the end, this protectionist policy has turned out to be profitable for the country."

"I can confirm this, Mr. President. Just between them, the three BAT musketeers—Baidu, Alibaba and Tencent—made a hundred or so acquisitions in 2015 totalling 16 billion US dollars, giving them the means to keep down any rising competition. On average, Chinese people spend 70% of their time on their cell phones, putting money into the coffers of the three companies: 55% to Tencent with its addictive games and its multifunction concierge WeChat, 10% to Alibaba for shopping, and 5% to Baidu in searching for websites. It would be impossible for any new arrival to break down the walls of this fortress!"

"Listen to this story. The boss of the Chinese subsidiary of one of our flagship groups in the environmental sector told me that, in order to get a contract from a large municipality, he organized a visit to one of his factories in France. The aim was to show the Chinese delegation that the company's excellence derived much more from its knowledge of project management that from its technological know-how, whose consistency was appreciated by everyone. But, in the evening, during a dinner held in a highly-renowned Paris restaurant, the head of the Chinese delegation told him that if he continued to conceal the technology that was being used, there was no chance of doing business. Result: the contract was never signed! I've also been told that one of our major groups providing services to the elderly opened its first retirement home in China last year. To the great surprise of the home's manager, on the very evening when it was opened, the People's Liberation Army came to tell him that he had 24 hours to leave the country. The manager had obtained all the necessary permits and tried to argue with them, but finally realized that he had been accused of stealing two members of staff from the Chinese army, which even a home-grown company would never have dared to do. He pleaded his good faith, saying that this could only have been done by chance, and that the 'fault' was not intentional. Then he finally realized where the root of the problem lay. In order to obtain official permission from the city, he had to state the job descriptions of each member of staff. The dossier was written in French in Paris, before being translated. With regard to kitchen staff, he mentioned the employment of two 'dishwashers' which, in the official Chinese document, became 'combat swimmers.'[4] The retirement home eventually opened, but it's worth remembering that the risk of 'lost in translation' is not an imaginary concept for anyone who wants to establish himself in China."

"Mr. President, I don't know if you are fond of Dalloyau's prepared foods—as Louis XIV was in his time—but it so happens that the company has just opened a splendid flagship in Hong Kong, all in marble. Their only surprise was to learn—only too

---

4   Presumably because, in French, a dishwasher is a *plongeur* and *plongeur* also means a diver.

late—that its name pronounced in Cantonese, the local dialect, means 'Fat butt'! Not easy in those circumstances to woo the Hong Kong *Tai tai* clientele ... There are hundreds of anecdotes like this, and I'm sure that the business leaders travelling with us have dozens of them to recount. China is country full of surprises. One of my friends works in micro-electronics in the Guangdong region. He recently came up against an unexpected problem on the production lines: the workers—mainly migrants—let one of their fingernails grow long so that, when they return to their native provinces, they can prove that they are no longer peasant farmers. As a result, they regularly scratch the components used on the assembly line. So never dismiss practical issues in China when it comes to implementing a business plan ..."

"So, put yourself in my shoes for a moment. What question would you ask the leaders I am going to meet, or what request would you make?"

"Mr. President, I would suggest above all that you ask for nothing ... If not, you'll be fighting a losing battle. In China, just be Chinese ..."

The New Digital Silk Road

"It's a bit late, don't you think? I'm not going get slant eyes or take to maotai, and fermented sorgho holds no attraction for me at all ... You know what the American journalist Dan Rather said when he sampled maotai during Richard Nixon's historic visit to Mao in 1972: 'It tastes not unlike liquid razor blades.' Just the very thought of it gives me a sudden desire for a cognac—to help prepare ourselves for the landing. We may be good republicans, but even so we should pay homage to royalty, so let's have them bring us a small carafe of Louis XIII ..."

"You understand me very well, Mr. President. Becoming Chinese means sharing their vision and raising oneself to the same level in terms of determination and courage. From their point of view, you represent two things that they find very attractive. You embody the French way of life which fascinates them, even if they will never adopt it lock stock and barrel and will 'sinicize' it to the degree they deem necessary. But you are also the leader of a great technological nation that is home to world-renowned companies with know-how they are in need of. They have clearly realized that the global game is turning in their favor. No one yet knows what will happen to the USA under the thumb of Donald Trump, and this uncertainty is itself a factor of weakness. Europe is in crisis and, as we said earlier, the Chinese have stopped thinking of it as a real power. On the other hand, China knows that France and Germany are two countries they can make alliances with in its duel with the new American administration. What does China need? Technology, as we have repeatedly said, but also intellectual resources that can be implemented to create new services and enrich its citizens' consumer experience. For Xi Jinping, there is a great deal at stake. He is in the middle of a ford that is crossing over to large scale economic and technological reform. To make the reform work, he needs us, because, if he fails, China will not achieve the productivity increases it needs in order to maintain the growth rate of its economy. And without growth, no jobs for new entrants to the labor market, no modernization of the welfare system, no money to finance pensions and healthcare infrastructure. So, the risk of mounting discontent among the population."

"I can see that, and I am quite prepared to adopt those guidelines—to propose we build a 'New Digital Silk Road' together, seeing as they like this type of grand design. Under the Trump administration, China could well find itself with restricted access to American technology. Let us offer our star technology companies the chance to take advantage of this and profit from the scale effect of the Chinese market. The USA has won the first round of the digital revolution hands down because of the size of their domestic market, so let us ally China with Europe and steal the second round from the USA—the round of the Internet of Things. We both have civilizations dating back a thousand years, so there has to be a way of getting along! However, I'm afraid we might be writing off the USA a bit too quickly. Despite Trump's declarations, the economic and commercial ties between the USA and China are close-knit and go back a long way. I don't see what either party would have to gain by pulling them apart ..."

"I'm sure you're right, Mr. President. The first reflex of the Chinese will always be to look towards the USA, but Donald Trump's unpredictable nature gives us a new card to play if we are clever enough. Look at the way Hermès went about it: for each 1,200 US dollar Apple Watch Hermès sold at the Sanlitun Apple Store in Beijing, 400 US dollars go to Apple and 800 to the French company ... A nice share-out of value, don't you think? In that same Apple Store, the Chinese would be surprised to discover that five out of every twelve of the highest-selling accessories are the product of French brains. This convinces me that we really do have a new role to play in China, aside from the major contracts. This includes the field of software which is, as I have said, a crucial sector for the Chinese. The Director of Human Resources at Criteo—a showpiece French company based in California whose business is the optimization of online advertising—told me that he gave preference to French people when recruiting staff. Firstly, because their level of schooling in pure mathematics is equal to the best American universities and this is a decisive factor in the production of the algorithms that are central to the business. Also, as he added, 'because the technology in our field is being reinvented every six months and there is nothing better than the devilishly critical French mind to tear apart any work done by someone else. And finally, because the French, who are used to dealing with both Lille and Marseille[5] know better than anyone how to adapt to environments with cultural differences.' Let me also remind you that the Huawei group has decided to install its main research centre outside China in Sophia Antipolis.[6] All this gives you some good conversation topics to use with the government leaders and bosses of large companies that you will be meeting."

The President turns to his communications adviser: "Anne, please, start arranging all that for the press conference we'll be having with President Xi Jinping in Beijing ... France as the principal contact for China in its technological revolution, as an alternative to the USA, the 'New Digital Silk Road' to outpace Germany ..."

"If you will allow me, Mr. President, may I advise you to act quickly? The Chinese won't wait for us; they are already poaching people from our research centers. Once the growth rate has started to recover, they'll think they don't need us any more."

The President calls Anne over once again: "Add too that our action in China comes when there is a window of opportunity which won't stay open forever. We only have this five-year mandate ahead of us, after which time China will no longer need us in order to deploy new digital technology in its own market, which is the largest in the world. We therefore have to act now and reach agreements before it's too late. When we land, call Jean-Pascal Tricoire for me—his France-China Committee will fine-tune all of that in specific statements for me when I get back to Paris."

"Of course I know that Jean-Pascal, as President of the Schneider Group, has been criticized for having been the first head of a CAC40 group to leave France and join you in Hong Kong.

---

5   i.e. with northerners and southerners in France
6   A technology park near Antibes in the south of France

During my campaign, I asked him what it would take for him to bring his head office back to Paris. He answered that only he and his family had moved; the head office was still in France. Anyway, this was no longer relevant for him, since the group has three operational head offices—in the USA, Europe and Asia—and he divides his time between the three. He brings his top executives together for one week every year and, the rest of the time, they remain in permanent contact with each other by digital means. There you have another Digital Silk Road ..."

"Since you have been kind enough to ask for my opinions, may I offer another piece of advice? The Chinese believe in shows of force. We must do the same and demand from them that the principle of reciprocity should operate, particularly with regard to direct investment. If we play at being the feeble rich pitched against the strong 'poor,' the outcome of any future negotiation is, unfortunately, a foregone conclusion. There is nothing to be gained from 'playing into China's hand'; contrary to what certain Western leaders have believed."

"You must be alluding to David Cameron who never understood that he would gain no more by prostrating himself before Xi Jinping than Tony Blair did with George Bush. In fact, Europe really began to fall behind in 2001 when China joined the World Trade Organization. The arrogance of the Clinton administration led Europe to impose no conditions on the Chinese as it was convinced that American products would flood the Chinese market. We all know what happened next ... Every time the West has been conciliatory towards China, either by arrogance or by submission, it has lost out! The Chinese have no such fear of negotiating with us. When I was a government minister, I remember what my Chinese counterpart said to me when I asked him to modify a contract that was under discussion: 'It's like a McDonald's franchise—take it or leave it!'"

"The Chinese proverb 'Eat bitter!' is quite a good indicator of how, in China, you can only win someone's respect if you show resistance. Once you have respect, exchanges can then become very fruitful. When Deng Xiaoping visited Lee Kuan Yew in Singapore in 1978, both countries' diplomats were concerned by an important problem of protocol: Deng had two deeply-rooted habits—he liked to smoke and to spit. This behavior was intolerable to Lee Kuan Yew—even chewing gum on the subway was subject to a fine in Singapore. The Singapore party ended up placing a spittoon next to Deng's armchair and a powerful smoke extractor was installed in the meeting room. The meeting lasted four hours, during which Deng neither smoked nor spit once ... A sign of the high respect in which he held the person whom he always regarded as his mentor."

"Who to trust when it comes to money?"

"I fully realize that one has to know how to enforce respect, like those wine producers from Burgundy you mentioned earlier! But today one has to admit that, whereas 'China eats bitter,' Europe can't get it up—if you will excuse my language! Discussions about granting China the status of a market economy bear witness to this. This issue is totally irrelevant, as the USA pointed out from the word go. In no sector does China allow market conditions to operate freely. Even when we claim we are getting tough—as in the case of excess capacity in steel production—we tax Chinese imports at 22% whereas the USA imposes a surtax of 500%! It is certainly praiseworthy to defend our steel mills, but wouldn't it be more judicious to concern ourselves primarily with the industries of the future, like access to the cloud, which has always been refused to foreign companies?"

"In my opinion, Mr. President, we have shown our weakness most in the field of mergers and acquisitions. That is the most flagrant illustration of the imbalance in the present power struggle with China. Whilst it is still almost impossible, *de facto*, for our French companies to make any significant acquisitions in China, Europe is like an open bar for Chinese predators. Look how your predecessors authorized the Dongfeng automobile group to take a 14% shareholding in the PSA group for only 850 million euros. With a seat on the Board, Dongfeng has access to the technological secrets of a company which, with over a thousand patents taken out every year, remains by far our national leader in research, all sectors included. How was it possible to give control of Toulouse airport to a Chinese—Mr. Poon—a man with a doubtful past, doubtful financing and not even squeaky-clean in the eyes of Beijing—when this infrastructure obviously has a critical value for our aeronautics industry, which is going to have to face up to future competition from China? During the same period, the Americans, through the intermediary of their powerful CFIUS—the Committee on Foreign Investment in the US—was applying itself to put a stop to the Chinese acquisition of key assets, as I mentioned before, or to demand sizeable additional premiums—as in the case of the operations of GE Appliances, bought by Haier for 5.4 billion US dollars after the Swedish company Electrolux had seen its bid of 3.4 billion killed off by the regulatory authorities. What's more, the Americans are trying to impose their rules on the rest of the world. They are taking the liberty of intervening in affairs being conducted between Europe and China, as in the case of the abortive attempt to sell Philips' lighting operations to its Chinese competitor."

"And yet, you must recognize that Europe began to wake up in autumn 2016, thanks to Germany. After the Vice-Chancellor, Sigmar Gabriel, having made the mistake of telling journalists during a trip to Beijing that he intended to give tins of black shoe polish to his Chinese counterparts to help them do their hair better, said that Chinese acquisitions in Germany would henceforth be subject to government approval in a wide range of industries."

"This is more a German approach than a European one, and it won't stop the Chinese from penetrating the Old Continent. It's also worth noting that, following Germany's initiative, the Chinese government announced a supposed self-limitation on Chinese investment abroad. In fact, this was just the formalization of unwritten rules that were already in force: China, through exchange control, has the right to oppose any acquisition of foreign assets by a Chinese company if this appears not to forward state interests and whose cost seems excessive, as in the Starwood affair which I mentioned earlier."

"Nevertheless we should rejoice in the fact that Europe is finally waking up thanks to Germany. But I agree, let us not be too optimistic in the conclusions we draw from the rise in our political power. To my mind, it's not a question of preventing China from investing in Europe. You yourself pointed out at the beginning of our conversation that this could be very useful and create wealth for Europe. It's a question of showing the Chinese that we cannot accept a one-way flow of investment. If our aim is to develop a common vision of the future with China, they must play the game of fair exchange, and accept that we too can make secure investments in Chinese businesses."

"Mr. President, use the example of the Pope in order to bring our two cultures closer together. In a historic interview he gave to the *Asian Times* magazine in 2015, he said: 'For me, China has always been a reference point of greatness.' In words like these, one senses the will to open the door to an accord between the official Catholic church and the underground church. As has always been the case in the past, discussions came up against a snag on the issue of the appointment of bishops, but one can see how, in face of their common enemy, Islamic State, the Vatican is prepared to water down—with holy water to boot—its communion wine."

"Yes, Pope Francis has already shown that he is ready to have some momentous meetings—for example, with the patriarch of the Orthodox Church in Cuba, the first such meeting since the schism of 1054."

"Indeed, Mr. President, the era lends itself to unprecedented reasoning. It's up to you to help to create some 'blue seas'—that marketing experts always talk about—between France and China. In other words, the creation of new markets by the bringing together of activities that have been separated in the past. This is what Puma instituted twenty years ago by associating sport and lifestyle. Today, fashion is associating itself with the feel good industries, making 'feel good' mean 'look good' too. The Cirque du Soleil brings together circus arts, music and theatre; fusion food is having great success in restaurants that are also art galleries by combining different culinary traditions from the whole world over; our food will become customized according to information provided by our DNA. In situations which appear to become blocked, like that of a market whose growth is slowing down, it is always by lateral thinking that new solutions are found."

"The idea of bringing together two major cultures, each with a thousand years of history, in order to celebrate them better, is something which really appeals to me!"

Once again, the President turns to Anne: "What if we organize a big party for the Chinese at Vaux-le-Vicomte with a candlelight dinner? Invite Sarkozy to be Master of Ceremonies and tell him it's going to be at Fouquet's! Sorry, just joking! Seriously though, call one of the few Frenchmen that the Chinese really respect: Alain Mérieux. And ask him what he would think of a Franco-Chinese summit in Paris to talk about our scientific and technical cooperation through the

*ages. Naturally, we would bring up the glorious moments of the past,
but also the future, and the ways to bridge our cultural differences ..."*

"Something like that would be very useful indeed, for some differences are occasionally difficult for Westerners to overcome. For example, in China, a signed contract is merely the equivalent of a letter of intent in our own legal framework. At any time, 'circumstances change, so the contract must change'; in other words, a contract signed at any given moment merely translates the balance of power of that moment. It can therefore evolve continuously. Two main notions can become misleading when you try to translate them: 'relationship' and 'face.' A 'relationship' in China takes much longer to establish itself, particularly with Westerners. Unfortunately this can take months or even years. However, once the relationship has been built up, it will be set in stone. This is what foreign businesses ignore completely by having their expats spend only two or three years in China, thereby condemning their mission to failure. My first question to any company boss who wants to set up business in China is whether he is ready to go there at least four times a year and, if on each occasion he can propose new product innovations, so as to keep his local partner motivated. The second notion is that of 'face,' which is much more important than in our country. In the West, congratulations offered to employees who are performing well are always welcome, but, in China, gratitude must be institutionalized in the form of a ceremony, preferably a dinner, and it must be made as official as possible."

"Valuable advice, to be sure. But you might be surprised at the number of times I am asked to intervene with regard to criminal practices that French companies have fallen victim to in China. Of course, I pass these on to our ambassador who doesn't quite know how to intervene ... It doesn't really help in bringing about any coming together of cultures ..."

"Not so surprising, Mr. President! We all have rather odd stories to tell. For example, one of my friends was visiting a company that was for sale in the south of China. While going round the offices, he noticed that the same staff member kept making an appearance from one department to another—a well-known way to make the purchaser believe that the company's operations are more extensive than they really are. Another example: a luxury French brand could not understand why it was losing its saleswomen a few months after they had been trained in the very best sales techniques for instilling customer loyalty. They would take down the personal details of customers so that the latter could benefit from the loyalty programme. It took the company some time before it realized that these employees were taking advantage of this to communicate directly with clients through their personal WeChat account and build up their own client portfolio which they would then take to a competitor in exchange for a considerable increase in salary! On a subtler level, one of my friends was encouraged to sell off an operation because he had been told it might be of potential interest to a state-owned enterprise. Sitting in Beijing on his own facing fifteen or so interlocutors across the desk, he began by quoting the price he was looking for. There followed an intense discussion between the members of the other side which ended thirty minutes later when, without any counter-argument, they turned to the translator with just one question: 'What is your counter-offer?' In a lighter vein, another of my friends was in a sales meeting with a prospective customer and was surprised to GET the reply that the latter had RECEIVED a more attractive offer from my friend's Chinese partner who, nevertheless, was subject to a non-compete clause. When the Chinese partner was questioned about what he had done, he replied: 'I'm not going into competition with you. I am simply offering our prospects the chance to choose.' I'll end my list of frustrations there ... Trust is indeed a rare commodity in China. The best thing is to apply the old American principle:

'God, we trust. All the others, we audit!' So, on a practical level, the most realistic solution from my point of view may appear the most counter-intuitive given what I have just told you: to make do with being a minority shareholder ..."

"But if you are a minority shareholder in China, I fear you will quickly end up like our bottle of Louis XIII: emptied of all your assets. Wasn't it Albert Frère who invented the saying 'Little minority, little fool; big minority, big fool!' Even Jack Ma, the head of Alibaba, much lauded in the Western press, behaved like a thug towards his fellow shareholders when, without warning, he took Alipay—its highly profitable online payment activity— away from Alibaba and put its control in the hands of a personal structure. He used the fallacious argument that the presence of foreign shareholders like eBay and Softbank no longer allowed him to keep the necessary administrative authorizations."

"Unfortunately, Mr. President, I can't promise you a joyride! But in a state where the rule of law does not prevail, the worst that can happen to you is to believe the law is on your side, especially as a majority shareholder. What has to be avoided is the 'Danone syndrome.' Danone discovered, in its joint venture with the beverage group Wahaha, the dangers of the absence of the rule of law. Because Danone did not understand this, it had to leave the water market, its tail between its legs. In the milk sector, Danone has now at least become a minority shareholder in the Chinese giant Mengniu, having brought to Mengniu its local operations after a devastating price war between almost fifteen hundred brands! Therefore, one is better off signing a 'one-sided treaty' recognizing that your local partner deserves goodwill for letting you get into the largest market in the world, even if you only get back a SHARE OF PROFITS that is lower than your true contribution. And if you produce innovations every quarter, at least the risk of being copied or expropriated is considerably reduced."

"Even so, one has to find the right partner. Musical chairs in China is not only played out to the tune of the Politburo of the Communist Party. What's more, among the private sector players in the field of new technology, positions can change very quickly. Xiaomi, who you have described as one of the unquestioned market leaders in low-cost smartphones, has seen its market share collapse recently. LeEco, a technology conglomerate whose operations range from digital television to electric cars, suddenly announced that they were having huge liquidity problems ... What advice can I then give to all the business leaders sitting there behind us in the plane to help them choose their Chinese partners with confidence?"

"Tell them it's not enough just to accompany you today. They have to come back to China on a regular basis. When making choices, the acid test is to ask whether two criteria have been met: integrity and sincerity, two pillars of Chinese values. Once these two tests have been passed, the business leaders should send representatives of their whole organization to China. The R&D Lab will have to bring in innovations every six months; The Finance Department will have to guarantee that, at each moment, the net cash exposure of the operations in the country conforms to what their Board of Directors previously authorized; Heads of Human Resources must recruit candidates for their attitude rather than their technical 'know-how,' so as to ensure their long-term attachment to the company; the Marketing Department may have to adopt the two-stage rocket principle, like Michelin who manages its premium Western brand for the high end of the market and a local brand for the rest of the market; as for the Legal Department, they will have to do intellectual gymnastics in order to handle situations that, for the most part, they will never have had to deal with before. Only one thing is certain: none of the normal working methods at head office in France can simply be replicated in China ... Finally, speaking more generally, your business leaders will have to promote a risk culture in a country where any venture is marked by trial and error over a long period. They should take their inspiration from the Singapore bank DBS, regularly earmarked as one of the best-managed banks in Asia. The Temasek sovereign fund, its largest shareholder, gave its support to the introduction of an Annual Failure Award. Each year, it rewards the experiment that has had management backing and, despite setbacks, has turned out to be a most worthwhile lesson that helps in thinking ahead to the future."

"You've given me one last idea there just before we land: perhaps I should introduce a 'Failure Prize' myself—for my ministers with regard to reform. After having made quite sure, of course, that my old friend Alain Juppé will not be competing!"

"So, Mr. President, since I see that we now have to fasten our seatbelts before touching down on the soil of Beijing, please allow me to thank you for these very free exchanges, and may I also ask you a favor? Might I conclude by suggesting one question to ask all of the ministers, advisers and top civil servants that you will work with during your mandate: 'As our companies are going to have to take a completely fresh look at themselves when they set up business in China, so how can we, the men and women in charge of reforming France, not draw some ideas from this country to help us reinvent ourselves?"

"Point well taken, my friend! During this flight, you have forecast not only changes in global equilibrium but also new political, economic and social models that will happen during my mandate. In a world of revolution, in search of new governance, I now have a better understanding of how China can be a sort of suggestions box. By taking the best ideas from the box, I can imagine how China can help us to remodel ourselves. You have strengthened me in my decision to make Beijing my first port of call as Head of State. But I won't go so far as to say that China will be a model for France to follow. To advance our history without compromising our culture remains the fundamental challenge of my mandate."

BACK TO 1850?

Beijing—The Temple Hotel—Post-discussum.

Gilbert Trigano, the brilliant founder of Club Méditerranée, which now flies the Chinese flag, had taken as his motto: 'I prefer a stupid idiot who can walk to ten intellectuals sitting down.' The Chinese are not just one, but one billion three hundred million and, what is more, they are anything but stupid. They do not walk, they run, and at a tempo that is now faster than the pace of everyone else on the planet. French intellectuals, meanwhile, continue to sit on Attali Commissions, which strive to make sure that the country will die cured. While France is mad about its think tanks, China deploys its 'action tanks.'

This is what makes one of my Shanghai friends say, 'In all the history of humankind, we are the only great civilization to have come back on top after disappearing. This feat is even more remarkable because, since 1978, we have been recovering faster than the speed at which we collapsed after 1850.' Historians should feel free to criticize the accuracy of this statement, but the important thing is that this is the feeling that now drives the Chinese.

Our old world, in which any new idea led to new business being created in the USA, to its pale imitation in China and to more regulations in Europe, has had its day. While, in the early years of this new century, the developed world is having problems reinventing itself, China, the spearhead of emerging countries, is inventing its future. It is fully embracing the motto 'Nothing quiet on the Eastern front,' by designing a political, economic and social system never seen before. The leadership of the Communist Party is contested not only by conservatives and reformers but also by the *Princelings*; the economy, led by the digital revolution and its new services, no longer lends itself to the same centralized dirigism as before; the emergence for the first time of real public opinion, born of 800 million Internet users, is bringing an end to preconceived ideas of a docile and easily controlled population.

Seen from outside, in a static way, it is true that China's situation has never seemed so fragile. Seen from inside, in a dynamic way, it has certainly never appeared so determined—the country seems ready to take up any challenge and the government seems to be willing to take on risks. However, any connaisseur of the Middle Kingdom will tell you that the shortest route never goes in a straight line. Reform will happen only in waltz step—meaning that it will regularly be taking two steps forward, then one step back. Chinese wisdom reminds us: 'The twisted tree lives out its life, the tree that grows straight ends up as planks.'

As is customary, it is a temptation for the West to take pleasure in every false step the Chinese make in reforming their system. Jack Ma, the iconoclastic founder of the giant company Alibaba, now the herald of the 'New China,' has already warned us: 'The next three to five years in China will be hard going.' It is up to us, then, as Europeans, to seize the opportunity of this narrow window and build a 'New Digital Silk Road' in more balanced conditions, by allying European technology with scale effects of the Chinese market. That will be the best way for Europe to reassert its presence in the second round of the digital revolution.

For it is certain that, if China wants to succeed in its radical transformation, it must not repeat the mistake it made in 1850 of withdrawing into itself. On the contrary, it must continue to draw inspiration from the best examples that exist in the rest of the world. It would be ironical if history repeated itself: if the West were also to close in on itself and sink into the same protectionism that led China into one hundred and fifty years of decline. This would give China free rein to take on the improbable role of defender of free trade and global prosperity in the new century!

Thus, just when the United Kingdom is leaving Europe and 'America is leaving America,' China can take pride in rediscovering 'THE China' of 1850.

On the other hand, the alternative for Europe will be to take inspiration from the pragmatism of the Middle Kingdom, which calls any schema into question if hard facts no longer prove it right. An echo, several centuries later, of what the prophet Mohammed said: "Go and seek out knowledge ... even in China!"

Hong Kong, December 2016.

david.baverez@pergamoncampus.com

ACKNOWLEDGMENTS

I thank Claudine, François and Pierre-Édouard,
my 'Three Magi,' and their precious gifts of advice.

www.ingramcontent.com/pod-product-compliance
Lightning Source LLC
Chambersburg PA
CBHW070928210326
41520CB00021B/6847